POETRY IN FOCUS

Canadian Cataloguing in Publication Data

Main entry under title:
Poetry in focus

For use in secondary schools.
Includes index.
ISBN 0-88996-066-6

1. Canadian poetry (English).* 2. English poetry.
3. American poetry. I. Cameron, Bob. II. Hogan, Margaret. III. Lashmar, Patrick.
PN6101.P63   821'.008   C82-095004-1

Printed and bound in Canada

15 14 13 12 11 10

Photographs:

Paul Till — cover photograph, pp.10-11, 26-27, 44-45, 68-69, 86-87, 100-101, 124-125.

Illustrations:

Harry Black — pp. 24, 40, 61, 82, 97, 121, 145.

Design:

Christine Alexiou

Editorial Services:

Dykeman, Tabor + Reeves-Stevens, Ltd.

Acknowledgements

The authors and publisher would like to thank the following people and organizations for permission to reproduce copyright material.

Page 12 — I Wonder How Many People in This City from THE SPICE BOX OF EARTH reprinted by permission of The Canadian Publishers, McClelland and Stewart Limited, Toronto; *The Sun Is Burning Gases (Loss of a Good Friend)* reprinted by permission of the author. *Page 13 — Tin Angel* © 1966 Siquomb Publishing Corporation. Used by permission. All rights reserved; *Johnnie's Poem* from BETWEEN TEARS AND LAUGHTER by Alden Nowlan © 1971 by Clarke, Irwin & Company Limited. Used by permission; *Thoughts on Silence* reprinted by permission of the author. *Page 14 — At Seventeen* Copyright ©1974, 1975 Mine Music Ltd., New York, N.Y. All Rights Reserved. *Page 15 — The Argument for Ascending* from HEADWATERS reprinted by permission of The Canadian Publishers, McClelland and Stewart Limited, Toronto. *Page 16 — Provincial* from DRIVING HOME by Miriam Waddington © Oxford University Press Canada; *Canoe Trip* reprinted by permission of the author. *Page 17 — 120 Miles North of Winnipeg* by Dale Zieroth, from CLEARING: POEMS FROM A JOURNEY (Toronto: House of Anansi Press, 1973). *Page 19 — The Long Voyage* Copyright 1938, renewal 1966 by Malcolm Cowley. From BLUE JUNIATA: COLLECTED POEMS (Viking, 1968); *Toronto Crossing* from POEMS by Robert Finch © Oxford University Press Canada; *Travel* from COLLECTED POEMS, Harper & Row. Copyright 1921, 1931, 1948, 1958 by Edna St. Vincent Millay and Norma Millay Ellis. *Page 20 — The Sound of Silence* © 1964,1965 Charing Cross Music Inc. *Page 21 — The Owl* Faber & Faber Ltd., publishers of COLLECTED POEMS by Edward Thomas and Myfanwy Thomas. Reprinted by permission of Myfanwy Thomas. *Page 22 — Riverdale Lion* from ABRACADABRA (1967), reproduced by permission of John Robert Colombo; *The Long Hill* Reprinted with permission of MacMillan Publishing Co., Inc. from COLLECTED POEMS by Sara Teasdale. Copyright 1920 by MacMillan Publishing Co., Inc., renewed 1948 by Mamie T. Wheless. *Page 24 — Dust of Snow* from CHIEF MODERN POETS OF BRITAIN AND AMERICA, 5th Edition. ED. Gerald DeWitt Sanders, John Herbert Nelson, & M.L. Rosenthal. MacMillan Company (Collier-MacMillan Ltd., London), 1970; *A Minor Bird* from CHIEF MODERN POETS OF BRITAIN AND AMERICA, 5th Edition. ED. Gerald DeWitt Sanders, John Herbert Nelson, and M.L. Rosenthal. MacMillan Company (Collier-MacMillan Ltd., London), 1970. *Page 25 — Birches, Fire and ice* From THE POETRY OF ROBERT FROST edited by Edward Connery Lathem. Copyright 1916,1923,1934 © 1969 by Holt, Rinehart and Winston, Copyright 1942,1944,1951 ©1962 by Robert Frost. Copyright © 1970 by Lesley Frost Ballantine. Reprinted by permission of Holt, Rinehart, and Winston, Publishers. *Page 46 — Heather Ale* Robert Louis Stevenson, "Heather Ale" in THE COMPLETE POEMS OF ROBERT LOUIS STEVENSON. Copyright 1923 Charles Scribner's Sons; copyright renewed (New York: Charles Scribner's Sons, 1923) Reprinted with the permission of Charles Scribner's Sons. *Page 47 — Waltzing Matilda* Copyright © 1936 by Allen & Co., Prop. Ltd. Melbourne, Australia. Copyright © 1941 by Carl Fischer, Inc. New York, Copyrights renewed. Reprinted by permission of Carl Fischer, Inc. *Page 48 — The Highwayman* by Alfred Noyes by permission of Hugh Noyes, for executor of the estate of Alfred

Noyes, St. Lawrence, Ventnor, Isle of Wight, England. *Page 52 — Cats in the Cradle* © 1974 Story Songs Ltd. (ASCAP). All rights reserved. *Page 53 — Ballad of Birmingham* Reprinted from POEM COUNTERPOEM, copyright © Dudley Randall. Reprinted by Permission of Dudley Randall. *Page 54 — The Times They Are A-Changin'* © MCMLXIII (UNP) by M. Witmark & Sons in the U.S.A. All rights reserved. *Page 58 — The Wreck of the Edmund Fitzgerald* © Moose Music Ltd., 1976. *Page 62 — The Shooting of Dan McGrew* from THE COLLECTED POEMS OF ROBERT SERVICE. Reprinted by permission of McGraw-Hill Ryerson, Limited, Reprinted by permission of DODD, MEAD & COMPANY, INC. from THE COLLECTED POEMS OF ROBERT SERVICE. Copyright 1907,1909,1912 by Dodd, Mead & Company Copyright 1916,1921 by Dodd, Mead and Company, Inc. Copyright 1940 by Robert Service. *Page 65 — Kathleen* Reprinted by permission of DODD, MEAD & COMPANY, INC. from MORE COLLECTED POEMS by Robert Service. Copyright 1949,1950,1951,1952,1953 by Dodd, Mead & Company Inc. *Page 67 — Comfort* from THE COLLECTED POEMS OF ROBERT SERVICE. Reprinted by permission of McGraw-Hill Ryerson Limited, Reprinted by permission of DODD, MEAD & COMPANY, INC. from THE COLLECTED POEMS OF ROBERT SERVICE. Copyright 1907,1909,1912 by Dodd, Mead & Company Copyright 1916,1921 by Dodd, Mead and Company, Inc. Copyright 1940 by Robert Service. *Page 71 — Riel* An excerpt from *Riel: A Poem for Voices* by Don Gutteridge. Reprinted with the permission of Nelson Canada. *Page 73 — Crucifixion* Lyrics and music by Phil Ochs © 1966 Barricade Music, Inc. (ASCAP) All rights administered by Almo Music Corp. (ASCAP) All rights reserved — International Copyright Secured. *Page 75 — Vincent (Starry, Starry Night)* © 1971 Mayday Music and The Benny Bird Co. Used by permission. All rights reserved. *Page 80 — At the Cedars* The work of Duncan Campbell Scott is reprinted with the permission of John G. Aylen, Ottawa. *Page 81 — The Execution* reprinted by permission of the author. *Page 83 — Disembarking at Quebec, The Planters, Death of a Young Son by Drowning* from THE JOURNALS OF SUSANNA MOODIE by Margaret Atwood © Oxford University Press Canada. *Page 84 — Progressive Insanities of a Pioneer* from THE ANIMALS IN THAT COUNTRY by Margaret Atwood © Oxford University Press Canada. *Page 88 — Life Lesson, Inevitability, Understanding* from LIKE HAIKU by Don Raye, copyright by Charles E. Tuttle Co., Inc., Tokyo, Japan; *New Year's Day, The Short Night, Giddy Grasshopper, Oh! I Ate Them All* from TO WALK IN SEASONS by William H. Cohen, copyright by Charles E. Tuttle Co., Inc., Tokyo, Japan. *Page 89 — Adversity* from LIKE HAIKU by Don Raye, copyright by Charles E. Tuttle Co., Inc., Tokyo, Japan; *The Warning* from VERSE, by Adelaide Crapsey. Copy 1922 by Algernon Crapsey and renewed 1950 by The Adelaide Crapsey Foundation. Reprinted by permission of Alfred A. Knopf, Inc. *Page 92 — On His Books* reprinted by permission of A.D. Peters & Co. Ltd.; *Wit* from THE COLLECTED POEMS OF IRVING LAYTON reprinted by permission of The Canadian Publishers, McClelland and Stewart Limited, Toronto. *Page 94 — cheerio my deario* Copyright 1927 by Doubleday & Company, Inc. from ARCHY AND MEHITABEL by Don Marquis. Reprinted by permission of the publisher.

(Acknowledgements continued on page 158.)

POETRY IN FOCUS

Bob Cameron
Margaret Hogan
Patrick Lashmar

Globe/Modern Curriculum Press
Toronto

Contents

New Directions 124

Introduction to Poetry

Poetry dates back in time to the misty beginnings of humanity. Even before there were established facts, people have been interested in the day-to-day existence of themselves and their fellows — survival, love, war, death, injustice, the universe. Throughout the centuries, people have found poetry to be a suitable outlet for expressing these sensations, emotions, and experiences. Whether in ballad, nursery rhyme, jingle, anthem, or modern-day song, people have found their intense and moving experiences to be most effectively expressed in poetry.

Advertisers, political campaign managers, and athletic cheering sections know the value of verse for catching on quickly, arousing enthusiasm, stimulating the imagination, and becoming imprinted indelibly on the mind. Verses learned at home, at school, and in the library become a life-long part of our lives.

Yet, despite its universal appeal over the centuries, poetry today certainly is not the most popular of literary genres. In school, it is too often introduced on the scholar's level, each poem being an intricate, sometimes inexplicable puzzle. When students think of poetry, they often think of strict rhyming patterns, difficult rhythmical conventions, complicated vocabulary, hidden meanings. Secondly, poetry is often regarded as being more difficult than prose.

These arguments are reasonable and should be dealt with. First of all, readers who enjoy poetry know that sometimes poetry *is* difficult. But they know that it is so only because it is fully involved with the inescapable complexities and uncertainties of existence. Poetry is one of the few guides that show how meaning and order are possible in a very complicated world. Just as astronauts explore the immensities above us, poets explore the immensities within us. They bring back new knowledge about the self, new and superior ways of feeling, and more accurate ways of seeing and interpreting the phenomena surrounding us. The fact of the matter is that the great mass of the world's poetry has been readily understood and smooth-flowing. Since its beginnings, and throughout most of the centuries of recorded time, poetry has been simple, easy to read and recite, and popular. It is hoped this book will help its readers understand and enjoy poetry as much as people have from the earliest times.

Sometimes poetry is more difficult to understand than prose. And certainly, the rhyme and rhythm play an integral part in a person's understanding of the poem. Also, because of the compression of thought, every word is important and must be understood. Sometimes readers must go beyond the literal meaning of words. They must be able to perceive the poem's meaning through suggested rather than direct statements. Therefore, what one person gets out of a poem may be quite different from the interpretation of his or her classmates or teacher.

In this individual aspect of poetry lies perhaps its greatest appeal. To share the experiences and feelings of another person, and to not have to find a "definitive" answer, is a great feeling. To be able to intelligently decide what one thinks, likes, and dislikes is what makes each of us an individual.

Poems are as different as are the people who read and who write them. Reading or writing a new poem is like meeting a new person — the experience itself makes the effort worthwhile.

1 Poetry is for Everyone

Poetry isn't solely a subject for analysis and study — it is an activity. You too can write poetry and maybe even have fun doing it! To write poetry you must let your natural responses, attitudes, and feelings come out in words. The life you are living is as meaningful to you as any "famous" person's life was or is to him or to her. Day in and day out, each of us is alternately fascinated and repelled by the variety of life — its sounds, colours, movements, and shapes. We feel, smell, taste, connect, discover — each of us is experiencing life. Therefore, each of us is capable of producing something heartfelt, intense, even marvelous. Each of us can produce one small phrase or many lines that are as perfect as any written by the poets featured in *Poetry in Focus*. The famous American poet, e. e. cummings, very clearly states his opinion on what qualities constitute a "poet."

> *A poet is somebody who feels, and who expresses his feelings through words.*
> *This may sound easy. It isn't.*
> *A lot of people think or believe or know they feel — but that's thinking or believing or knowing; not feeling. And poetry is feeling — not knowing or believing or thinking.*
> *Almost anybody can learn to think or believe or know, but not a single human being can be taught to feel. Why? Because whenever you think or you believe or you know, you're a lot of other people: but the moment you feel, you're nobody-but-yourself.*

Poetry, then, is for everyone. For this reason, *Poetry in Focus* will present many diverse poems — poems written by people from different cultures, people of different nationality, age, education, and historical era. Throughout the text and in this chapter, particularly, we will find that many people have excelled in the writing of poetry. And perhaps through the lessons and activities in this text, you will find that you yourself are capable of composing something of which you are proud, something that has meaning for you.

I Wonder How Many People in This City
Leonard Cohen

I wonder how many people in this city
live in furnished rooms.
Late at night when I look out at the buildings
I swear I see a face in every window
looking back at me,
and when I turn away
I wonder how many go back to their desks
and write this down.

The Sun is Burning Gases (Loss of a Good Friend)
Cathleen McFarland

I was young when
17 was a number
Too high to count
The sun was the miracle
Spinning sorcerer
That melted my crayons
Into bright wax rivers.
A golden-skinned princess lived there
Nightly in my mind,
When stars and moon
were marginal connect-the-dots,
different everytime —
Beyond the realms of man.

Now I'm 17
And even infinity is
A place I can define.
Man has touched the moon —
Now stretching to the stars.
I know the sun is burning gases
My princess long since turned to ashes.

Tin Angel
Joni Mitchell

Varnished weeds in window jars
Tarnished beads on tapestries
Kept in satin boxes are
Reflections of love's memories

Letters from across the seas
Roses dipped in sealing wax
Valentines and maple leaves
Tucked into a paperback

Guess I'll throw them all away
Found someone to love today

Dark with darker moods is he
Not a golden Prince who's come
To columbines and wizardry
To talk of castles in the sun

Still I'll take a chance and see
I found someone to love today

There's a sorrow in his eyes
Like the angel made of tin
What will happen if I try
To place another heart in him

In a Bleeker Street cafe
I found someone to love today
I found someone to love today

Johnnie's Poem
Alden Nowlan

Look! I've written a poem!
Johnnie says
and hands it to me
            and it's about
            his grandfather dying
            last summer, and me
            in the hospital
and I want to cry,
don't you see, because it doesn't matter
if it's not very good:
            what matters is he knows
and it was me, his father, who told him
            you write poems about what
            you feel deepest and hardest.

Thoughts on Silence
Mary Jane Sterling

What am I doing here
Among these strange people
Sitting in these funny desks
Staring at this paper?
Oh yes, I am in school.
These people are my classmates.
Though they chatter all the time
They are silent now.
Now I can think.
I see a bird flying high in the air.
Maybe it is flying south.
My heart leaps with the bird
Taking a message to my mother.
My mind is heavy, thinking something sad has
Happened at home.
But the birds are singing
Everything is all right.
The breeze has whispered something in my ear.
I hope it whispers the same joyous words to my people.
I get lonely for my family and I especially miss my mother
But I shall see them all soon.
When we meet we won't even touch hands
But our hearts will leap with joy
And in our minds we will be glad.

At Seventeen

Janis Ian

I learned the truth at seventeen
That love was meant for beauty queens
— And high school girls with clear skinned smiles
Who married young and then retired.
The valentines I never knew,
The Friday night charades of youth
Were spent on one more beautiful —
At seventeen I learned the truth.

And those of us with ravaged faces
Lacking in the social graces,
Desperately remained at home
Inventing lovers on the phone
Who called to say, "Come dance with me,"
And murmured vague obscenities.
It isn't all it seems,
At seventeen.

A brown-eyed girl in hand-me-downs
Whose name I never could pronounce
Said, "Pity, please, the ones who serve,
They only get what they deserve.
The rich relationed home-town queen
Marries into what she needs
A guarantee of company
And haven for the elderly."

Remember those who win the game
Lose the love they sought to gain
In debentures of quality
And dubious integrity.
Their small town eyes will gape at you
In dull surprise when payment due
Exceeds accounts received,
At seventeen.

To those of us who know the pain
Of valentines that never came,
And those whose names were never called
When choosing sides for basketball.
It was long ago and far away,
The world was younger than today,
And dreams were all they gave for free
To ugly duckling girls like me.

We all play the game and when we dare
To cheat ourselves at solitaire
Inventing lovers on the phone,
Repenting other lives unknown,
That call and say, "Come dance with me,"
And murmur vague obscenities
At ugly girls like me
At seventeen.

Focus on Meaning

1. From what you have learned of poetry in past grades, discuss whether Cohen's poem "I Wonder How Many People in This City" is in fact a poem. What is the author trying to say?

2. Discuss what you feel the poems "The Sun is Burning Gases (Loss of a Good Friend)" and "Thoughts on Silence" are about. Are these poems specific to the girls in the poems or are they expressing common human experiences? Explain.

3. Accurate word-sketches of objects, people, and feelings occur frequently in Joni Mitchell's work. Write a short character description of the speaker in "Tin Angel." How old is she, what problem confronts her, what decision does she make regarding this problem?

4. What is the speaker of "Johnnie's Poem" revealing about life? Do you agree with this philosophy?

5. a) With the poem "Thoughts on Silence" in mind, write an example of how you think a government, perhaps with the best of intentions, has oppressed a minority group.
   b) Write an example of how you or another individual, either with the best of intentions or unknowingly, have oppressed some other individual.

6. Janis Ian's poem "At Seventeen" shows many of the problems and complexities of growing up. Do you find adolescence a particularly trying time? Why or why not?

2 Prose and Poetry

Generally, it is fairly easy to distinguish between prose and poetry.

Because poetry has a number of distinct and definite forms, most people can tell that a poem is a poem simply by looking at it. There is a break at the end of each line in poetry; prose is constructed of sentences. In poetry, a number of lines forms a stanza; in prose, a number of sentences forms a paragraph. A poem has other external signs that identify it: a rhyme scheme, a regular stanza pattern, capital letters at the beginning of many lines. True, some modern poetry does not conform to all of these standard conventions, but most poetry does.

Perhaps the most obvious distinguishing feature between prose and poetry is rhythm. Rhythm can be defined as the regular recurrence of stressed and unstressed syllables in a line. A poem contains words arranged in a rhythmic pattern. That is, in poetry (except for free verse), the accents of the syllables in the words fall at regular intervals. Although most poets allow themselves some freedom in accents, they stay within a rhythmic pattern. It is not hard to find the regular poetic feet in the structure of most poems. The prose line, on the other hand, almost always contains a mixture of accented and unaccented syllables without any pattern or regularity. Some prose (e.g. many passages from the novels of D. H. Lawrence and James Joyce) is fairly rhythmical. However, we do not ordinarily call such passages poems.

Another important difference between prose and poetry is the use of imagery. When words are used to cause us to see, hear, touch, taste, or smell something, they are creating an image. Since poetry is a very compact mode of expression, concentrated images or image patterns are often used to help the reader form a total impression. Although not all poetry relies heavily on the use of images, it is safe to say that most poetry does. Much of the enjoyment of poetry comes from responding to the visual and aural suggestions in a poem, and to the imagery that appeals to our other senses.

The Argument for Ascending
Sid Marty

Sidehill gouging
gives your ankles pain
stiffkneed evenings
and arthritic old age

Slabrock and ice
have let so many down
from an awkward balance
to their finger ends
The mystery of falling

Gravity too, is my domain
It turns you, swimmer, over
I watch from the steep approaches

Would you be the man for the mountain?
The skulls of goats, the skulls of sheep
    foot my precipitous fences

Learn to fail sometimes, bear with me

    Your body is the cross you carry
up to the high places

And your reward
a tearing wind
a view

of endless higher mountains

Provincial
Miriam Waddington

My childhood
was full of people
with Russian accents
who came from
Humble Saskatchewan
or who lived in Regina
and sometimes
visited Winnipeg
to bring regards
from their frozen
snowqueen city.

In those days
all the streetcars
in the world slept
in the Elmwood
car-barns and the
Indian moundbuilders
were still wigwammed
across the river
with the birds
who sang in the bushes
of St. Vital.

Since then I have
visited Paris
Moscow London
and Mexico City
I saw golden roofs
onion domes and the
most marvellous
canals, I saw people
sunning themselves
in Luxembourg Gardens
and on a London parkbench
I sat beside a man
who wore navy blue socks
and navy blue shoes
to match.

All kinds of miracles:
but I would not trade
any of them for the
empty spaces, the
snowblurred geography
of my childhood.

Canoe Trip
Douglas Le Pan

What of this fabulous country
Now that we have it reduced to a few hot hours
And sun-burn on our backs?
On this south side the countless archipelagoes,
The slipway where titans sent splashing the last great
    glaciers;
And then up to the foot of the blue pole star
A wilderness,
The pinelands whose limits seem distant as Thule,
The millions of lakes once cached and forgotten,
The clearings enamelled with blueberries, rank silence
    about them;
And skies that roll all day with cloud-chimeras
To baffle the eye with portents and unwritten myths,
The flames of sunset, the lions of gold and gules.
Into this reservoir we dipped and pulled out lakes and
    rivers,
We strung them together and made our circuit.
Now what shall be our word as we return,
What word of this curious country?

It is good,
It is a good stock to own though it seldom pays dividends.
There are holes here and there for a gold-mine or a hydro-
    plant.
But the tartan of river and rock spreads undisturbed,
The plaid of a land with little desire to buy or sell.
The dawning light skirls out its independence;
At noon the brazen trumpets slash the air;
Night falls, the gulls scream sharp defiance;
Let whoever comes to tame this land, beware!
Can you put a bit to the lunging wind?
Can you hold wild horses by the hair?
Then have no hope to harness the energy here,
It gallops along the wind away.
But here are crooked nerves made straight,
The fracture cured no doctor could correct.
The hand and mind, reknit, stand whole for work;
The fable proves no cul-de-sac.
Now from the maze we circle back;
The map suggested a wealth of cloudy escapes;
That was a dream, we have converted the dream to act.
And what we now expect is not simplicity,
No steady breeze, or any surprise,
Orchids along the portage, white water, crimson leaves.
Content, we face again the complex task.

And yet the marvels we have seen remain.
We think of the eagles, of the fawns at the river bend,
The storms, the sudden sun, the clouds sheered downwards.
O so to move! With such immaculate decision!
O proudly as waterfalls curling like cumulus!

120 Miles North of Winnipeg
Dale Zieroth

My grandfather came here years ago,
family of eight. In the village,
nine miles away, they knew him as
the German and they were suspicious, being
already settled. Later he was
somewhat liked; still later
forgotten. In winter everything
went white as buffalo bones and
the underwear froze on the line
like corpses. Often the youngest
was sick. Still he never thought
of leaving. Spring was always greener
than he'd known and summer had
kid-high grass with sunsets big
as God. The wheat was thick,
the log house chinked and warm.
The little English he spoke
he learned from the thin grey lady
in the one-room school, an hour away
by foot. The oldest could hunt, the youngest
could read. They knew nothing of
the world he'd left, and forgotten,
until 1914 made him an alien and
he left them on the land he'd come to,
120 miles north of Winnipeg.

Focus on Meaning

1. a) Both "The Argument for Ascending" and "Canoe Trip" present individuals involved in challenging themselves and nature. What is the similarity of their experiences?
   b) With Marty's poem "The Argument for Ascending" in mind, present a brief argument in favour of some sport you enjoy, such as hockey, water skiing, skiing, or horseback riding. Be sure to include mention of the dangers, the advantages, and the main reason you participate in this particular sport.

2. a) Discuss what the poet is saying in the poem "Provincial." Do you have the same feelings as those expressed by the speaker of this poem?
   b) With this poem in mind, recreate in a paragraph or two an incident from your childhood that is still charged with emotion.

3. a) Why was the grandfather in "120 Miles North of Winnipeg" made an alien in the year 1914?
   b) Having read Zieroth's "120 Miles North of Winnipeg," discuss whether you feel that people's reactions to newcomers have changed in the last seventy-five years.

4. In thinking back to our childhood days, each of us remembers some of the things that happened and forgets others. What sorts of events do you think people tend to remember? Why?

5. In many cultures there are coming-of-age ceremonies that leave childhood behind and declare a person an adult. How would you define an adult in our society? The criteria may be privileges, responsibilities, or physical capacities. What happens when these do not occur together but are spread out over a long period of time and occur in random order?

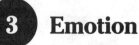

3 Emotion

Genuine poetry is spontaneous. It springs from a deeper level of the self than we're aware of in daily life. Every true poem is generated by the dynamo of emotional experience, though it may take this emotion a long time to break through into the world of conscious thinking. Therefore, although a finished poem is a combination of feeling and thinking, it originates in the deep, inexplicable wells of emotion.

Emotional experience more than anything else is what poetry gives us. And this is what we value as much as anything in life. Our lives are afloat on seas of emotion. We live there more richly than we live in any geographical world. T.S. Eliot once commented, "The poet who 'thinks' is merely the poet who can express the emotional equivalent of thought."

We all know an emotion when we feel one. We know that strong emotion has a marked and instant physical effect on us. It influences our heartbeat, our breathing, and the distribution of our blood flow (we flush or grow pale). It is no wonder that poetry affects sensitive readers in a physical way. Emily Dickinson judged poetry by its physical effect:

If I read a poem and it makes my whole body
so cold no fire can ever warm me I know that
is poetry. If I feel physically as if the top of my
head were taken off, I know that is poetry.
These are the only ways I know it . . . .

We do not have to believe in the ideas of a poem to share its experience. But we do have to believe in its emotions. Our emotions are so many and so complex that we can hardly classify them. Yet these emotions, though sometimes mixed, can remain distinct.

It is quite possible for a poem to have too much emotion. Emotion in excess of its object is called "sentimentality." Run-of-the-mill poetry often is guilty of sentimentality — emotion gone out of control and taking over.

Emotion is healthy when it is of the kind and in the amount that its object deserves: when what we love is really lovable, when what we fear is really fearful. Sentimentalists are less concerned with the object of their emotion than with the fact that they themselves are feeling it. Writers of sentimental poetry like to play on our stock responses — those built-in automatic reactions we have to many things we think dear and familiar: home, sweet home; childhood; old rocking chairs; motherhood; the fidelity of dogs. It was no doubt the sentimentalists' doting views on children and dogs that led W. C.

Fields, a lifelong crusader against sentimentality in life, to overreact with his famous pronouncement: "Nobody who hates dogs and little children can be all that bad."

Therefore the emphasis in a poem may not be its hidden meaning, its ulterior purpose. Many poems simply reflect the moods and thoughtful moments that everyone has. Young people even more than older people are subject to a wide variety of moods — sometimes joyful, sometimes sad, sometimes pensive. The thoughts that grow out of these moods are often serious ones. Loneliness, for example, may trouble you from time to time, and you might find yourself trying to work out in your mind your relationship with others. At other times, you might feel a desire to travel, a need for freedom, a sense of jubilation. All these feelings, and many more, are a combination of outward and inward influences, often too complicated to explain but always very real.

The poems in this book (and particularly in this chapter) reflect a number of moods, and may cause you to reflect upon things you perhaps haven't yet had time to think about very much. Do not be surprised, however, if you find that most of the poems describe moods and emotions that you have already felt but have never put clearly into words.

Invictus

William Ernest Henley

Out of the night that covers me,
   Black as the Pit from pole to pole,
I thank whatever gods may be
   For my unconquerable soul.

In the fell clutch of circumstance
   I have not winced nor cried aloud.
Under the bludgeonings of chance
   My head is bloody, but unbowed.

Beyond this place of wrath and tears
   Looms but the horror of the shade,
And yet the menace of the years
   Finds, and shall find me, unafraid.

It matters not how strait the gate,
   How charged with punishments the scroll,
I am the master of my fate:
   I am the captain of my soul.

The Long Voyage

Malcolm Cowley

Not that the pines were darker there,
nor mid-May dogwood brighter there,
nor swifts more swift in summer air;
   it was my own country,

having its thunderclap of spring,
its long midsummer ripening,
its corn hoar-stiff at harvesting,
   almost like any country,

yet being mine; its face, its speech,
its hills bent low within my reach,
its river birch and upland beech
   were mine, of my own country.

Now the dark waters at the bow
fold back, like earth against the plow;
foam brightens like the dogwood now
   at home, in my own country.

Toronto Crossing

Robert Finch

The well-drest woman in the costly car
Stares at the busfolk waiting in the wet,
The soldiers thumbing rides; her cigarette
Impeccably finds where lighter and ashtray are.

The well-drest car round the costly woman purrs
At its quiver of light shopping, its corner full
Of the new books, its driver a furred fruit on wool;
The purr the car purrs is both its and hers.

If she were those people waiting, she wouldn't, she'd walk.
This has been an unusually exhausting day.
The lights have been against her all the way.
She flicks her unfinished smoke onto the sidewalk
As the lights change and the changed eyes of the starer
Release the crowd for a double glance at the mirror.

Travel

Edna St. Vincent Millay

The railroad track is miles away,
   And the day is loud with voices speaking,
Yet there isn't a train goes by all day
   But I hear its whistle shrieking.

All night there isn't a train goes by,
   Though the night is still for sleep and dreaming,
But I see its cinders red on the sky,
   And hear its engine steaming.

My heart is warm with the friends I make,
   And better friends I'll not be knowing;
Yet there isn't a train I wouldn't take,
   No matter where it's going.

The Sound of Silence
Paul Simon

Hello darkness my old friend,
I've come to talk with you again,
Because a vision softly creeping,
Left its seeds while I was sleeping
And the vision that was planted in my brain
Still remains within the sound of silence.

In restless dreams I walked alone,
Narrow streets of cobble stone
'Neath the halo of a street lamp,
I turned my collar to the cold and damp
When my eyes were stabbed by the flash of a neon light
That split the night, and touched the sound of silence.

And in the naked light I saw
Ten thousand people maybe more,
People talking without speaking,
People hearing without listening,
People writing songs that voices never share
And no one dares disturb the sound of silence.

"Fools!" said I, "You do not know
Silence like a cancer grows
Hear my words that I might teach you
Take my arms that I might reach you."
But my words like silent raindrops fell
And echoed, in the wells of silence.

And the people bowed and prayed
To the neon God they made,
And the sign flashed out its warning
In the words that it was forming.
And the sign said:
    "The words of the prophets are written
    on the subway walls and tenement halls"
And whispered in the Sounds of silence.

Focus on Meaning

1. In "Invictus," is the speaker's claim to being "master" of his fate supported in the poem? In what kind of life situations can people demonstrate that they are "masters" of their souls?

2. What would you consider the theme of "The Long Voyage" to be? Explain.

3. In a few seconds, the speaker of "Toronto Crossing" observes and sums up the character of the driver. From the moment the light turns red until the car moves away with the next green light, the poet has developed a negative picture of this person. Supporting your answer with references to the poem, write a character sketch of the driver.

4. The call of distant places sometimes can be very loud, especially when life seems to grow monotonous. In "Travel," Edna St. Vincent Millay does not say exactly where she would like to go — she speaks only of the desire to see new places and have new experiences. If you could travel wherever you wished, where would it be? Why do you want to go there?

5. a) What emotion is present in "The Sound of Silence"? Have you ever experienced it? How did you deal with it?
   b) Find some poems in this text in which someone uses emotion as an escape from a reality he or she cannot face. Discuss the ways in which emotion is used.

6. a) Sentimentality, which gives free access to unearned emotions, is at home in the popular arts — the movies, TV, best-selling fiction, advertising — which show us not the world as it is but the world as magically transformed to what we would like it to be. What objects do you think you yourself tend to be sentimental about? Let yourself write a frankly sentimental prose paragraph about such an object.
   b) Then rewrite your paragraph so that, while still heartfelt, it has no traces of sentimentality.

7. With the poems from this chapter in mind, write a mood paragraph on one of the following: life, death, love, hate, loneliness, destruction, faith, doubt, people, courage, eternity, fear, or wishes.

# 4 Purpose

The smallest meaningful part of the poem is the word. But a single word already contains within itself more than an unwary reader might suspect. The basic elements of a poem — image, sound, and meaning — may all be found in the isolated word. Of course, these elements acquire richness and precision when the word is placed in the context of other words. The study of poems is necessarily a close examination of the surrounding words that modify and influence any particular word. The fabric of words that is the poem depends on the strength, colour, and texture of each individual thread.

A word has a physical nature (its vowel and consonant structure), a history (its origin and the later changes in its usage), a "family life" (kinships and affinities with other words), and a future (the new and unpredictable life that the poet and others can give to it). These are the conditions that affect the word's power to radiate image, sound, and meaning.

All poetry has meaning. In the previous chapters we looked at poems with a fairly obvious surface meaning. However, many poems have deeper meanings, meanings which the reader must search out. The poems in this chapter all have hidden meanings and you, the reader, must be prepared to read these poems very carefully in order to derive this ulterior, beneath-the-surface purpose.

The Owl
Edward Thomas

Downhill I came, hungry, and yet not starved;
Cold, yet had heat within me that was proof
Against the North wind; tired, yet so that rest
Had seemed the sweetest thing under a roof.

Then at the inn I had food, fire, and rest,
Knowing how hungry, cold, and tired was I.
All of the night was quite barred out except
An owl's cry, a most melancholy cry

Shaken out long and clear upon the hill,
No merry note, nor cause of merriment,
But one telling me plain what I escaped
And others could not, that night, as in I went.

And salted was my food, and my repose,
Salted and sobered, too, by the bird's voice
Speaking for all who lay under the stars,
Soldiers and poor, unable to rejoice.

Riverdale Lion
John Robert Colombo

Bound lion, almost blind from meeting their gaze and popcorn
the Saturday kids love you. It is their parents
who would paint your mane with polkadots to match their
   California shirts
and would trim your nails for tieclips.

Your few roars delight them. But they wish you would quicken
   your pace
and not disappear so often into your artificial cave
for there they think you partake of secret joys and race
through the jungle-green lair of memory
under an African sun as gold as your mane.

But you fool them. You merely suffer the heat and scatter the
   flies
with your tail. You never saw Africa.
The sign does not tell them that you were born here, in
   captivity,
that you are as much a Canadian as they are.

The Long Hill
Sara Teasdale

I must have passed the crest a while ago
   And now I am going down —
Strange to have crossed the crest and not to know,
   But the brambles were always catching the hem of my gown.

All the morning I thought how proud I should be
   To stand there straight as a queen,
Wrapped in the wind and the sun with the world under me —
   But the air was dull, there was little I could have seen.

It was nearly level along the beaten track
   And the brambles caught in my gown —
But it's no use now to think of turning back,
   The rest of the way will be only going down.

When I Heard the Learn'd Astronomer
Walt Whitman

When I heard the learn'd astronomer,
When the proofs, the figures, were ranged in columns before me,
When I was shown the charts and diagrams, to add, divide, and
    measure them,
When I sitting heard the astronomer where he lectured with much
    applause in the lecture-room,
How soon unaccountable I became tired and sick,
Till rising and gliding out I wander'd off by myself,
In the mystical moist night air, and from time to time,
Look'd up in perfect silence at the stars.

Focus on Meaning

1. With Edward Thomas's poem "The Owl" in mind, conduct an oral interview with someone you know who has had an encounter with a wild animal. If the storyteller uses vivid descriptions, catchy phrases, dialogue, or dialect, try to retain as many of the interesting descriptive words or phrases as possible. Pretend that you are this person and convert the experience into a short story.

2. "Riverdale Lion" is ostensibly about a lion, but the poem also contains a few veiled comments about man. Taking this statement into account, discuss what you feel the meaning of this poem to be.

3. Sara Teasdale's poem also contains two levels of meaning. Apparently, the speaker has climbed a "long hill," realizes she has passed the crest, and is now on her way down the hill.

   With this surface meaning in mind, what is the second level of meaning in "The Long Hill"?

4. No direct statement of the speaker's viewpoint in "When I Heard the Learn'd Astronomer" is made, but his viewpoint is suggested. What do you think the speaker is really implying in this poem?

5. Discuss the presentation of reality in one of the poems in this chapter. Do you agree with the ideas presented in the poem? Do these ideas apply to "real life"? Why?

Robert Frost was born in San Francisco, but was really a displaced New Englander, for his family had lived in New England since 1632. By the time he was ten they moved to Massachusetts, and for most of the rest of his life, Frost lived in the New England area. It is this area which is the background or inspiration for much of his poetry.

When Frost graduated from high school, he and a young girl named Elinor White shared the honours of the valedictory address. Far from being a situation of jealousy or competition — it was love. They were married three years later, in 1895. For the first two years of their marriage, Frost worked mainly as a teacher, then entered Harvard but wasn't happy as a student. He wanted to work and write poetry. With this in mind, he bought a farm and supported his family by farming and teaching until 1912. Little of the poetry he wrote during this time was published. In 1912, Elinor encouraged him to make a change. They sold the farm and moved their four children to England where they lived until 1915. Ironically, for someone who would become the most famous of American poets, his work was accepted first in England. Critics there raved about his first two books, *A Boy's Will* (1913) and *North of Boston* (1914). By the time Frost returned to the United States, he was famous at home as well. He then bought more farmland in New England and lived there, alternating his time on the farm with time spent in teaching positions at various colleges and universities. Above all, he kept on writing poetry. His life continued in this way until his death.

Robert Frost received four Pulitzer Prizes for his poetry — the only poet ever to achieve that distinction. Why is he praised so highly as a poet? His poetry makes the truth understandable. He may criticize the world, but it is very clear that he also loves the world.

Dust of Snow

The way a crow
Shook down on me
The dust of snow
From a hemlock tree

Has given my heart
A change of mood
And saved some part
Of a day I had rued.

A Minor Bird

I have wished a bird would fly away,
And not sing by my house all day;

Have clapped my hands at him from the door
When it seemed as if I could bear no more.

The fault must partly have been in me.
The bird was not to blame for his key.

And of course there must be something wrong
In wanting to silence any song.

Birches

When I see birches bend to left and right
Across the lines of straighter darker trees,
I like to think some boy's been swinging them.
But swinging doesn't bend them down to stay.
Ice-storms do that. Often you must have seen them
Loaded with ice a sunny winter morning
After a rain. They click upon themselves
As the breeze rises, and turn many-colored
As the stir cracks and crazes their enamel.
Soon the sun's warmth makes them shed crystal shells
Shattering and avalanching on the snow-crust —
Such heaps of broken glass to sweep away
You'd think the inner dome of heaven had fallen.
They are dragged to the withered bracken by the load,
And they seem not to break; though once they are bowed
So low for long, they never right themselves:
You may see their trunks arching in the woods
Years afterwards, trailing their leaves on the ground
Like girls on hands and knees that throw their hair
Before them over their heads to dry in the sun.
But I was going to say when Truth broke in
With all her matter-of-fact about the ice-storm
I should prefer to have some boy bend them
As he went out and in to fetch the cows —
Some boy too far from town to learn baseball,
Whose only play was what he found himself,
Summer or winter, and could play alone.
One by one he subdued his father's trees
By riding them down over and over again
Until he took the stiffness out of them,
And not one but hung limp, not one was left
For him to conquer. He learned all there was
To learn about not launching out too soon
And so not carrying the tree away
Clear to the ground. He always kept his poise
To the top branches, climbing carefully
With the same pains you use to fill a cup
Up to the brim, and even above the brim.
Then he flung outward, feet first, with a swish,
Kicking his way down through the air to the ground.
So was I once myself a swinger of birches.
And so I dream of going back to be.
It's when I'm weary of considerations,
And life is too much like a pathless wood
Where your face burns and tickles with the cobwebs
Broken across it, and one eye is weeping
From a twig's having lashed across it open.

I'd like to get away from earth awhile
And then come back to it and begin over.
May no fate willfully misunderstand me
And half grant what I wish and snatch me away
Not to return. Earth's the right place for love:
I don't know where it's likely to go better.
I'd like to go by climbing a birch tree,
And climb black branches up a snow-white trunk
Toward heaven, till the tree could bear no more,
But dipped its top and set me down again.
That would be good both going and coming back.
One could do worse than be a swinger of birches.

Fire and Ice

Some say the world will end in fire,
Some say in ice.
From what I've tasted of desire
I hold with those who favor fire.
But if it had to perish twice,
I think I know enough of hate
To say that for destruction ice
Is also great
And would suffice.

Focus on Robert Frost

1. Robert Frost says that poetry "makes you remember what you didn't know you knew." Do you think this statement fits any of the poems in this first unit? Does it fit Frost's poems?

2. a) In what kinds of ways do people escape from the routine or the stress of daily life? Which of these ways do you think are effective? for others? for you? Do you think they would be effective for Robert Frost? Explain.
    b) Frost says, "One could do worse than be a swinger of birches." What is your comment on this?

3. Robert Frost's poems reflect a minute observation of the landscape. Where do you especially see this in the poems here? Which poem best shows his familiarity with and love of nature?

4. Frost claims that a poem should begin in delight and end in wisdom. What does he mean? Which of the poems here do you think follow this plan?

Tales from Long Ago

Traditional ballads are songs that tell a simple story or tale. They are one of the earliest forms of folk literature. These ballads were as popular in the fourteenth to sixteenth centuries as popular music is today. Some modern poems and many modern songs have much in common with traditional ballads.

The authorship of these old ballads is unknown but there are many theories about how they were composed. It is believed that these story poems were composed by ordinary people who could neither read nor write. It is likely that wandering singers and court minstrels composed many ballads. Others were probably composed by a group of people. In any case, the authors of traditional ballads were people with very little formal education.

Traditional ballads were in the oral tradition. This means they were not written down but rather were passed from one area to another and from one generation to the next by word of mouth. Due to the imagination of the individual balladeer, lapses in memory, and local differences, a ballad frequently had numerous versions.

Eventually, many of these ballads were collected and published by Bishop Thomas Percy in 1765 and Sir Walter Scott in the early nineteenth century. Many story poems were thus preserved in books for future generations to enjoy. There is no way of knowing how many were lost.

Traditional ballads are part of the early literature of most countries. The early settlers in North America from such countries as England, Scotland, and Ireland brought a diverse collection of traditional ballads with them. Soon they began to change some of them to fit their new situation. They also composed their own.

English, Scottish, Irish, and North American traditional ballads are still enjoyed today. Singers such as Joan Baez, Judy Collins, Ian Tyson, and Peter, Paul, and Mary recorded many of these during the early 1960s and many of these recordings are still available today. Most recently, traditional ballads have been recorded by Ryan's Fancy and numerous others.

All of the poems in this unit are traditional ballads. They all have a story to tell. They provide us with insights into the lives of our ancestors.

5 Tales of the Supernatural

The modern world is fascinated with the supernatural. We enjoy the mystery and the strong emotional response elicited by supernatural stories and events. Evidence of strong interest and outright belief in things supernatural is all around us. Many sports coaches believe in good luck charms such as particular hats or specific ties. We can have our palms read or, if we prefer, have our tea leaves read by numerous "psychic professionals."

Did you ever stop to think how often the theme of the supernatural appears in modern novels and movies? Look at the movie and television listings in your local newspaper to note how often this theme occurs. At your favourite bookstore, note the number of modern novels built around supernatural themes. The supernatural has a market.

For all our sophistication, we still are drawn to the supernatural. The mystery, the curiosity, the hidden power, and the potential for greater knowledge that all lurk in the frightening depths of night still are very much with us.

This strong attraction to the supernatural is an important theme running through the literature of every age.

The novel *Frankenstein* terrified readers in the nineteenth century. Some of the most memorable as well as chilling moments in Shakespearean drama are the witches' scenes in *Macbeth* and the ghost and graveyard scenes in *Hamlet*. The terrible one-eyed Cyclops was but one of a wide array of monsters, gods, and goddesses that dominated Greek and Roman mythology.

Perhaps the Middle Ages was a time when people's belief in the power of the supernatural was strongest. This period is also known as the Dark Ages, a time when most people were very poor, illiterate peasants. For these people, ghosts and devils were real; medieval peasants burnt witches. As a result, it is natural to see evidence of a strong belief in magic and the supernatural in the literature of this period. Many traditional ballads from this period — and all of the ballads in this chapter — are mysterious tales of the supernatural.

The Unquiet Grave
Anonymous

"The wind doth blow today, my love,
    And a few small drops of rain;
I never had but one true-love,
    In cold grave she was lain.

"I'll do as much for my true-love
    As any young man may;
I'll sit and mourn all at her grave
    For a twelvemonth and a day."

The twelvemonth and a day being up,
    The dead began to speak:
"O who sits weeping on my grave,
    And will not let me sleep?"

"'Tis I, my love, sits on your grave,
    And will not let you sleep;
For I crave one kiss of your clay-cold lips,
    And that is all I seek."

"You crave one kiss of my clay-cold lips;
    But my breath smells earthy strong;
If you have one kiss of my clay-cold lips,
    Your time will not be long.

"'Tis down in yonder garden green,
    Love, where we used to walk,
The finest flower that e'er was seen
    Is withered to a stalk.

"The stalk is withered dry, my love,
    So will our hearts decay;
So make yourself content, my love,
    Till God calls you away."

Thomas the Rhymer

Anonymous

True Thomas lay on Huntlie bank;
    A ferlie he spied wi' his e'e;
And there he saw a ladye bright
    Come riding down by the Eildon Tree.

Her skirt was o' the grass-green silk,
    Her mantle o' the velvet fyne;
At ilka tett o' her horse's mane,
    Hung fifty siller bells and nine.

True Thomas he pu'd aff his cap,
    And louted low down on his knee:
'Hail to thee, Mary, Queen of Heaven!
    For thy peer on earth could never be.'

'O no, O no, Thomas,' she said,
    'That name does not belang to me;
I'm but the Queen o' fair Elfland,
    That am hither come to visit thee.

'Harp and carp, Thomas,' she said;
    'Harp and carp along wi' me;
And if ye dare to kiss my lips,
    Sure of your bodie I will be.'

'Betide me weal, betide me woe,
    That weird shall never daunten me.'
Syne he has kiss'd her rosy lips,
    All underneath the Eildon Tree.

'Now ye maun go wi' me,' she said,
    'True Thomas, ye maun go wi' me;
And ye maun serve me seven years,
    Thro' weal or woe as may chance to be.'

She's mounted on her milk-white steed,
    She's ta'en true Thomas up behind;
And aye, whene'er her bridle rang,
    The steed gaed swifter than the wind;

O they rade on, and farther on,
    The steed gaed swifter than the wind;
Until they reach'd a desert wide,
    And living land was left behind.

'Light down, light down now, true Thomas,
    And lean your head upon my knee;
Abide ye there a little space,
    And I will show you ferlies three.

'O see ye not yon narrow road,
    So thick beset wi' thorns and briers?
That is the Path of Righteousness,
    Though after it but few inquires.

'And see ye not yon braid, braid road,
    That lies across the lily leven?
That is the Path of Wickedness,
    Though some call it the Road to Heaven.

'And see ye not yon bonny road
    That winds about the fernie brae?
That is the Road to fair Elfland,
    Where thou and I this night maun gae.

'But, Thomas, ye sall haud your tongue,
    Whatever ye may hear or see;
For speak ye word in Elfyn-land,
    Ye'll ne'er win back to your ain countrie.'

O they rade on, and farther on,
    And they waded rivers abune the knee;
And they saw neither sun nor moon,
    But they heard the roaring of the sea.

It was mirk, mirk night, there was nae starlight,
    They waded thro' red blude to the knee;
For a' the blude that's shed on the earth
    Rins through the springs o' that countrie.

Syne they came to a garden green,
    And she pu'd an apple frae a tree:
'Take this for thy wages, true Thomas;
    It will give thee the tongue that can never lee.'

'My tongue is my ain,' true Thomas he said;
    'A gudely gift ye wad gie to me!
I neither dought to buy or sell
    At fair or tryst where I might be.

'I dought neither speak to prince or peer,
    Nor ask of grace from fair ladye!' —
'Now haud thy peace, Thomas,' she said,
    'For as I say, so must it be.'

He has gotten a coat of the even cloth,
    And a pair o' shoon of the velvet green,
And till seven years were gane and past,
    True Thomas on earth was never seen.

The Wife of Usher's Well
Anonymous

There lived a wife at Usher's well,
    And a wealthy wife was she;
She had three stout and stalwart sons,
    And sent them o'er the sea.

They hadn't been a week from her,
    A week but barely one,
When word came to the aged wife
    That her three sons were gone.

They hadn't been a week from her,
    A week but barely three,
When word came to the aged wife
    That her sons she'd never see.

"I wish the wind may never cease,
    Nor troubles from the flood,
Till my three sons come home to me
    In earthly flesh and blood!"

It fell about the Martinmas,
    When nights are long and dark,
The aged wife's three sons came home,
    And their hats were made of bark.

It neither grew in marsh nor ditch,
    Nor yet in any slough;
But at the gates of Paradise
    That bark full freely grew.

"Blow up the fire, my maidens!
    Bring water from the well!
For at my house we'll feast tonight
    Since my three sons are well."

And she has made for them a bed,
    She's made it large and wide;
And she's taken her mantle her about,
    Sat down at the bedside.

Up then crew the red, red cock,
    And up and crew the gray;
The eldest to the youngest said,
    "'Tis time we were away."

The cock he hadn't crow'd but once,
    Nor clapped his wings that day,
When the youngest to the eldest said,
    "Brother, we must away."

"The cock does crow, the day does dawn,
    The channerin' worm does chide;
If we be miss'd out of our place,
    A sore pain we must bide."

"Lie still, lie still but a little wee while,
    Lie still but if we may;
If my mother should miss us when she wakes,
    She'll go mad ere it be day."

"Fare you well, my mother dear!
    Farewell to barn and byre!
And fare you well, the bonny lass
    That kindles my mother's fire!"

Focus on Meaning

1. Many traditional ballads contain elements of the supernatural. What unnatural things occurred in each poem? List several modern stories you know of that contain similar supernatural elements.

2. Literature dealing with supernatural events often is "spooky" in tone. List words and phrases from the poems in this chapter that help develop the effect of "spookiness."

3. Ballads often make heavy use of dialogue. Who are the speakers in the imagined conversation in each poem?

4. There are many different versions of each traditional ballad. Modern versions of ballads use modern English. Older versions contain words no longer used in modern English. Rewrite one of the poems in this chapter using modern-day English.

5. A ballad only gives a very brief outline of the story being told. The details are left to the reader's or listener's imagination. List the main events in one of the poems in this chapter. Now add some details to each of the main events on your list. Compare your list with that of a partner.

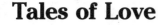

6 Tales of Love

The art of falling in love is not a recent phenomenon. The theme of romantic love is the most common theme running through literature. The various love themes are so familiar, one wonders what more can be said about love. Listen to the radio, watch television, play the albums in your collection, or read any poetry anthology and you will see how common is the theme of romantic love in its various forms. Lovers are imprisoned by love, enchanted by love, made complete by love, and made lonely by love. Love in these poems, stories, and songs can mean passion or pain, contentment or despair. It can be a promise for tomorrow or be the stuff that memories are made of.

The new poets and songwriters continue to rework the well-known love themes, bringing fresh understanding and delight to the reader or listener. They employ modern images and ideas but the results are the same. Love has made the world "go 'round" for as long as people can remember and such is still the case today.

You have loved and do love so you know a great deal about it already. Through literature you can experience the love of others and thus gain for yourself new insights into its mysteries. Characters in literature delight in love, despair in love, give all for love, and even die for love. Many traditional ballads, like many modern songs, are love stories. Many of them are tragic tales of love gone wrong while others tell of love ending in bliss. Read the love stories from long ago in this chapter. Note that the joys and perils of loving are no different today from those of the past.

Barbara Allan
Anonymous

It was in and about the Martinmas time,
    When the green leaves were a-falling,
That Sir John Graeme in the west country
    Fell in love with Barbara Allan.

He sent his man down through the town,
    To the place where she was dwelling,
"O haste and come to my master dear,
    Gin ye be Barbara Allan."

O hooly, hooly rose she up
    To the place where he was lying,
And when she drew the curtain by —
    "Young man, I think you're dying."

"O it's I am sick, and very, very sick,
    And 'tis a' for Barbara Allan,"
"O the better for me ye's never be,
    Tho' your heart's blood were a-spilling.

"O dinna ye mind, young man," said she,
    "When ye was in the tavern a-drinking,
That ye made the healths gae round and round,
    And slighted Barbara Allan?"

He turned his face unto the wall,
    And death was with him dealing:
"Adieu, adieu, my dear friends all,
    And be kind to Barbara Allan."

And slowly, slowly raise she up,
    And slowly, slowly left him;
And sighing, said she could not stay,
    Since death of life had reft him.

She was not gane a mile but two,
    When she heard the dead-bell ringing,
And every jow that the dead-bell geid,
    It cry'd, "Woe to Barbara Allan!"

"O mother, mother, make my bed,
    O make it soft and narrow,
Since my love died for me today,
    I'll die for him tomorrow."

Scarborough Fair

Anonymous

Are you going to Scarborough Fair?
Parsley, sage, rosemary and thyme;
Remember me to one that lives there,
For once she was a true love of mine.

Tell her to make me a cambric shirt,
Parsley, sage, rosemary and thyme;
Without any seam or fine needlework,
And then she'll be a true love of mine.

Tell her to wash it in yonder dry well,
Parsley, sage, rosemary and thyme;
Where water ne'er sprung, nor drop of rain fell,
And then she'll be a true love of mine.

Tell her to dry it on yonder thorn,
Parsley, sage, rosemary and thyme;
Which never bore blossom since Adam was born,
And then she'll be a true love of mine.

O, will you find me an acre of land,
Parsley, sage, rosemary and thyme;
Between the sea foam and the sea sand
Or never be a true lover of mine.

Oh, will you plough it with a lamb's horn,
Parsley, sage, rosemary and thyme;
And sow it all over with one peppercorn,
Or never be a true lover of mine.

Oh, will you reap it with a sickle of leather,
Parsley, sage, rosemary and thyme;
And tie it all up with a peacock's feather,
Or never be a true lover of mine.

And when you have done and finished your work,
Parsley, sage, rosemary and thyme;
Then come to me for your cambric shirt,
And you shall be a true love of mine.

Lord Randall

Anonymous

"Where have you been all the day, Randall, my son?
Where have you been all the day, my pretty one?"
"I've been to my sweetheart's, mother;
I've been to my sweetheart's, mother;
Please make my bed soon.
For I'm sick to the heart and I fain would lie down."

"What have you been eating there, Randall, my son?
What have you been eating there, my pretty one?"
"Eels and eel's broth, mother;
Eels and eel's broth, mother;
Now make my bed soon,
For I'm sick to the heart and I fain would lie down."

"What was the color of their skins, Randall, my son?
What was the color of their skins, my pretty one?"
"Spickle and sparkle, mother;
Spickle and sparkle, mother;
Now make my bed soon,
For I'm sick to the heart and I fain would lie down."

"Where did she get them from, Randall, my son?
Where did she get them from, my pretty one?"
"From hedges and ditches, mother;
From hedges and ditches, mother;
Now make my bed soon,
For I'm sick to the heart and I fain would lie down."

"What will you leave your family, Randall, my son?
What will you leave your family, my pretty one?"
"My gold and my silver, mother;
My gold and my silver, mother;
Please make my bed soon,
For I'm sick to the heart and I fain would lie down."

"What will you leave your sweetheart, Randall, my son?
What will you leave your sweetheart, my pretty one?"
"A rope to hang her, mother;
A rope to hang her, mother;
Now make my bed soon,
For I'm sick to the heart and I fain would lie down."

The Gypsy Rover
Anonymous

The gypsy rover come over the hill,
Bound through the valley so shady;
He whistled and he sang till the green woods rang,
And he won the heart of a lady.

Chorus:
Ha di do, ah dido da day,
Ah di do, ah di day dee;
He whistled and he sang till the green woods rang,
And he won the heart of a lady.

She left her father's castle gate,
She left her own true lover;
She left her servants and her estate,
To follow the gypsy rover.

Her father saddled his fastest steed,
Roamed the valley all over;
Sought his daughter at great speed,
And the whistling gypsy rover.

He came at last to a mansion fine,
Down by the river Clayde;
And there was music, and there was wine,
For the gypsy and his lady.

He's no gypsy, my father, said she,
My lord of freelands all over;
And I will stay till my dying day,
With my whistling gypsy rover.

Focus on Meaning

1. As you know, ballads are also songs. Look for recorded arrangements of the ballads in this chapter. Learn to sing some of them. Perhaps you might set the other ballads in this chapter to music of your own. In groups, you might want to perform these ballads for the class.

2. Because ballads are simple stories they often leave out details. Readers or listeners can only imagine what these details might be.
   a) Read the poem "Barbara Allan" and list at least three questions that are left unanswered in the poem. Now, using your imagination and the facts from the poem, compose answers to these questions.
   b) In the poem "Lord Randall," we are not told why Lord Randall has been poisoned by his sweetheart. Write a story telling why you think she poisoned him.

3. What is the mood in "The Gypsy Rover"? List several words or phrases which suggest this feeling in the poem. How does it compare with the mood of the other poems in this chapter?

4. With a group, prepare a dramatic presentation of one of the scenes from one of the ballads in this unit. You might like to use choral speaking, movement, dialogue, simple props, and sound effects. Your group could write a short script, rehearse, and present the scene to the class or another class in the school. The dialogue used in the poem may help you write the dialogue in your script.

5. List the name of a modern novel, movie, or television program that tells of a tragic story of two lovers. In what ways is the story similar to the one in the poem? How is it different?

What do William Lyon MacKenzie and Benedict Arnold have in common? For one thing, both men were considered traitors to their countries. William Lyon MacKenzie gained notoriety by leading the ill-fated Rebellion in Upper Canada in 1837 while Benedict Arnold became known as a traitor by "selling out" to the British during the American Revolutionary War. Such treachery to one's country is known as treason. Historically, traitors have been punished more severely than enemies for their faithlessness, usually by death.

Treachery is a part of our lives. Being "turned in" by a friend when one has done something wrong is often considered a treacherous act by the friend. The betrayal of our trust wounds us most when the traitor is a close friend or a relative. At one time or another we have all been let down by friends or relatives. Treachery is not surprising coming from enemies but such acts by trusted friends and kin are rarely anticipated and hurt deeply.

Treachery is a common theme in traditional ballads. The ballads in this chapter tell of several tragic tales of treachery. As you study these poems, try to think of similar modern-day examples of treachery.

Johnie Armstrong
Anonymous

There dwelt a man in faire Westmerland,
   Johnie Armstrong men did him call,
He had nither lands nor rents coming in,
   Yet he kept eight score men in his hall.

He had horse and harness for them all,
   Goodly steeds were all milke-white;
O the golden bands about their necks,
   And their weapons, they were all alike.

Newes then was brought unto the king
   That there was sicke a won as hee,
That livèd lyke a bold out-law,
   And robbèd all the north country.

The king he writt a letter then,
   A letter which was large and long;
He signed it with his owne hand;
   And he promised to doe him no wrong.

When this letter came Johnie untill,
   His heart it was as blythe as birds on the tree:
"Never was I sent for before any king,
   My father, my grandfather, nor none but mee.

"And if wee goe the king before,
   I would we went most orderly;
Every man of you shall have his scarlet cloak,
   Lacèd with silver laces three.

"Every won of you shall have his velvett coat,
   Laced with silver lace so white;
O the golden bands about your necks,
   Black hatts, white feathers, all alyke."

By the morrow morninge at ten of the clock,
   Towards Edenburough gon was hee,
And with him all his eight score men;
   Good Lord, it was a goodly sight for to see!

When Johnie came befower the king,
   He fell downe on his knee;
"O pardon, my soveraine leige," he said,
   "O pardon my eight score men and mee!"

"Thou shalt have no pardon, thou traytor strong,
   For thy eight score men nor thee;
For tomorrow morning by ten of the clock,
   Both thou and them shall hang on the gallow-tree."

But Johnie looke'd over his left shoulder,
   Good Lord, what a grievous look looked hee!
Saying, "Asking grace of a graceless face —
   Why there is none for you nor mee."

But Johnie had a bright sword by his side,
   And it was made of the mettle so free,
That had not the king stept his foot aside,
   He had smitten his head from his faire bodde.

Saying, "Fight on, my merry men all,
   And see that none of you be taine;
For rather then men shall say we were hange'd,
   Let them report how we were slaine."

Then, God wott, faire Edenburough rose,
  And so besett poore Johnie rounde,
That fowerscore and tenn of Johnie's best men
  Lay gasping all upon the ground.

Then like a mad man Johnie laid about,
  And like a mad man then fought hee,
Untill a falce Scot came Johnie behinde,
  And runn him through the faire bodde.

Saying, "Fight on, my merry men all,
  And see that none of you be taine;
For I will stand by and bleed but awhile,
  And then will I come and fight againe."

Newes then was brought to young Johnie Armstrong,
  As he stood by his nurse's knee,
Who vowed if ere he live'd for to be a man,
  On the treacherous Scots reveng'd hee'd be.

The Golden Vanity
Anonymous

There was a gallant ship, a gallant ship was she,
And the name of the ship was "The Golden Vanity,"
And they feared she would be taken by the
    Turkish enemy
  As she sailed upon the Lowland, Lowland, Lowland,
  As she sailed upon the Lowland sea.

Then up came a little cabin boy, and thus spoke he,
Speaking to the captain, "What will you give to me
If I swim alongside of the Turkish enemy
  And sink her in the Lowland, Lowland, Lowland,
  And sink her in the Lowland sea?"

"I'll give you an estate in the North Countrie,
And my one and only daughter your lovely bride
    shall be,
If you'll swim alongside of the Turkish enemy
  And sink her in the Lowland, Lowland, Lowland,
  And sink her in the Lowland sea."

Then the boy made ready and overboard sprang he,
And swam alongside of the Turkish enemy,
And with his auger sharp in her side he bored
    holes three,
  And he sunk her in the Lowland, Lowland, Lowland,
  He sunk her in the Lowland sea.

Then the boy swam around, and back again swam he,
And he called to the captain of "The Golden Vanity."
But the captain mocked, "You can drown for all of me!"
  And he left him in the Lowland, Lowland, Lowland,
  He left him in the Lowland sea.

The boy swam around, he came to the port side,
He looked up at his messmates, and bitterly he cried:
"Oh, messmates, take me up, for I'm drifting
    with the tide,
  And I'm sinking in the Lowland, Lowland, Lowland,
  I'm sinking in the Lowland sea."

His messmates took him up, but on the deck he died,
And they sewed him in a hammock that was so
    large and wide.
They lowered him overboard, but he drifted
    with the tide,
And he sank beneath the Lowland, Lowland, Lowland,
He sank beneath the Lowland sea.

Whiskey in the Jar
Anonymous

As I was a-goin' over Gilgary Mountain,
I met Colonel Pepper and his money he was countin'.
I drew forth my pistol and I rattled out
        my sabre saying:
"Stand and deliver for I am a bold deceiver."

Chorus:

>   Mush-a-rig-gum dur-um dye.
>   Whack fol di dad-dy-o,
>   Whack fol di dad-dy-o,
>   There's whiskey in the jar.

Those gold and silver coins they sure did
        look inviting;
So I picked up the money and I took it home to Molly.
She promised and she swore that she never
        would deceive me;
But the Devil's in the women and they never
        can be easy.

When I awoke, 'twas between six and seven,
The guards they were around me, in numbers
        odd and even.
I sprang for my pistols, but alas I was mistaken;
For Molly took my pistols and prisoner I was taken.

They threw me in jail, without a judge or writin',
For robbin' Colonel Pepper on that damn
        Gilgary Mountain.
But they didn't take my fists, so I knocked
        the sentry down,
And bid a fond farewell to that jail in Salem town.

Now, some take delight in fishing and in bowling,
Others take delight in the carriages a-rolling.
But I take delight in the juice of the barley,
And courtin' pretty maidens in the morning,
        bright and early.

Focus on Meaning

1. Like many traditional ballads, "Johnie Armstrong" is based on historical fact. The Border country between England and Scotland was an area of constant fighting between the Scots and the English in the sixteenth century. Johnie Armstrong was an English Border raider who was tricked into visiting King James V of Scotland and who was subsequently slain.
   a) In groups of four, discuss whether King James V acted correctly in tricking and killing the "outlaw" and his men. Take just ten minutes to discuss this and to record your ideas.
   b) Select one member of the group to present your ideas to the rest of the class.

2. Since traditional ballads were passed down through the oral tradition, there are many versions of traditional ballads. Many of the versions of "The Golden Vanity" have different endings. In one, the captain awards the estate but refuses to give up his daughter. Think of another way this ballad could have ended.

3. "Whiskey in the Jar" has been recorded many times. Bring a recording of this ballad to class and listen to the beat and melody. Note how these conform to the rhythm of the poem.
   a) Try to set one of the other ballads in this chapter to music. Do this individually or in small groups. Begin by reading the ballad aloud. Get the feel of the rhythm. Experiment with various melodies until you come up with one to fit stanza one. Use that melody for the other stanzas.
   b) Share your musical version of the ballad you chose with others in your class.

4. Treachery is still common today. Examine a recent newspaper and list several examples of modern-day treachery that are reported there. Share and discuss your examples with a partner. Do you always agree on whether some action is treacherous or not? How does point of view affect one's interpretations of what is and is not treacherous?

8 Tales from a Young North America

The early settlers to North America brought with them far more than just axe blades and ploughs, traps and fishing nets. The main component of their baggage was their culture. The newcomers brought with them their political, social, and religious beliefs and institutions. With them also came their art, their music, and their literature. And so, a rich collection of traditional ballads was transplanted in the New World.

Because this folk literature was in the oral tradition, numerous new versions of old Scottish, English, Welsh, French, and Irish ballads were developed in the widely disparate pockets of western civilization that emerged all across North America. Naturally the new situations in the New World gave rise to many new story songs. Soon there were thousands of ballads indigenous to North America that were sung by the common folk as they had been sung by their ancestors in their homeland. These early North American songs were sung in the fishing villages, on the farms, in the logging camps, and in the mills, the mines, and the factories. These early ballads told of the adventures of loggers, the perils of a life at sea, the ruggedness of the wild west, and the troubles of the worker.

The Poor Little Girls of Ontario
Anonymous

I'll sing you a song of that plaguey pest,
It goes by the name of the Great North-West.
I cannot have a beau at all,
They all skip out there in the fall.

Refrain: One by one they all clear out,
        Thinking to better themselves, no doubt,
        Caring little how far they go
        From the poor little girls of Ontario.

First I got mashed on Charlie Brown,
The nicest fellow in all the town.
He tipped his hat and sailed away,
And now he's settled in Manitobay.

Then Henry Mayner with his white cravat,
His high stiff collar and his new plug hat,
He said if he stayed he'd have to beg,
And now he's settled in Winnipeg.

Then my long-legged druggist with his specs
   on his nose,
I really thought he would propose,
But he's sold his bottle-shop and now he's gone
Clear out to little Saskatchewan.

I'll pack my clothes in a carpet sack,
I'll go out there and I'll never come back,
I'll find me a husband and a good one, too,
If I have to go through to Cariboo.

Last refrain: One by one we'll all clear out,
        Thinking to better ourselves, no doubt,
        Caring little how far we go
        From the old, old folks of Ontario.

Come All You Bold Canadians

Anonymous

Come all you bold Canadians, I'd have you lend an ear
Concerning a fine ditty that would make your courage cheer,
Concerning an engagement that we had at Sandwich town,
The courage of those Yankee boys so lately we pulled down.

There was a bold commander, brave General Brock by name,
Took shipping at Niagara and down to York he came,
He says, "My gallant heroes, if you'll come along with me,
We'll fight those proud Yankees in the west of Canaday!"

'Twas thus that we replied: "Along with you we'll go,
Our knapsacks we will shoulder without any more ado.
Our knapsacks we will shoulder and forward we will steer;
We'll fight those proud Yankees without either dread or fear."

We travelled all that night and a part of the next day,
With a determination to show them British play.
We travelled all that night and a part of the next day,
With a determination to conquer or to die.

Our commander sent a flag to them and unto them did say:
"Deliver up your garrison or we'll fire on you this day!"
But they would not surrender, and chose to stand their ground,
We opened up our great guns and gave them fire a round.

Their commander sent a flag to us, for quarter he did call.
"Oh, hold your guns, brave British boys, for fear you slay us all.
Our town you have at your command, our garrison likewise."
They brought their guns and grounded them right down before our eyes.

And now we are all home again, each man is safe and sound.
May the memory of this conquest all through the Province sound!
Success unto our volunteers who did their rights maintain,
And to our bold commander, brave General Brock by name!

Jesse James
Anonymous

It was on a Wednesday night, the moon was
   shining bright,
  They robbed the Glendale train.
And the people they did say, from near and far away,
  'Twas the outlaws Frank and Jesse James.

Refrain:
      Jesse had a wife to mourn all her life,
        The children they are brave.
      'Twas a dirty little coward shot Mister Howard,
        And laid Jesse James in his grave.

It was Robert Ford, the dirty little coward,
  I wonder how he does feel,
For he ate of Jesse's bread and he slept in Jesse's bed,
  Then he laid Jesse James in his grave.

It was his brother Frank that robbed the Gallatin bank,
  And carried the money from the town.
It was in this very place that they had a little race,
  For they shot Captain Sheets to the ground.

They went to the crossing not very far from there,
  And there they did the same;
And the agent on his knees he delivered up the keys
  To the outlaws Frank and Jesse James.

It was on a Saturday night, Jesse was at home
  Talking to his family brave,
When the thief and the coward, little Robert Ford,
  Laid Jesse James in his grave.

How people held their breath when they heard
   of Jesse's death,
  And wondered how he ever came to die
'Twas one of the gang, dirty Robert Ford,
  That shot Jesse James on the sly.

Jesse went to his rest with his hand on his breast.
  The devil will be upon his knee.
He was born one day in the county of Clay,
  And came from a solitary race.

Nova Scotia: A New Ballad
Anonymous

Let's away to *New Scotland*, where Plenty sits queen
O'er as happy a country as ever was seen;
And blesses her subjects, both little and great,
With each a good house, and a pretty estate.
  Derry down, (down, down, derry down).

There's wood, and there's water, there's wild fowl
   and tame;
In the forest good ven'son, good fish in the stream,
Good grass for our cattle, good land for our plough
Good wheat to be reap'd, and good barley to mow.
  Derry down, etc.

No landlords are there the poor tenants to teaze,
No lawyers to bully, nor stewards to seize:
But each honest fellow's a landlord, and dares
To spend on himself the whole fruit of his cares.
  Derry down, etc.

They've no duties on candles, no taxes on malt,
Nor do they, as we do, pay sauce for their salt:
But all is as free as in those times of old,
When poets assure us the age was of gold.
  Derry down, etc.

Focus on Meaning

1. a) In "The Poor Little Girls of Ontario," why were the young men of Ontario moving to the North-West? Why do young people today often move from one part of Canada to another?
   b) Write a newspaper ad for the Canadian government in 1890, encouraging young people to settle in the North-West.

2. The courage of Canadian and British soldiers under the leadership of General Brock is recounted in this ballad. Are the facts in this ballad presented in an unbiased way? Was there a clear victor in the War of 1812?

3. Write a newspaper account of the murder of Jesse James or of the battle in "Come All You Bold Canadians." Make sure your news story answers the 5 W's of good report writing.

4. The ballad "Nova Scotia: A New Ballad" appeared in England around 1750 just after the new pioneer town of Halifax had been established. The author had a purpose for composing this ballad. What do you think it was?

Sir Walter Scott was born in Edinburgh, Scotland in 1771. He spent many of his boyhood years living on his grandparents' farm at Sandyknowe in Border country. There he became immersed in the history, the legends, and the poetry of the colourful Border area between Scotland and England. He spent many a day learning Border ballads from his grandparents. His passion for the romance of the Border country never left him. As a student at Edinburgh University and later, as a young lawyer, he made many trips to Border country absorbing the history and folk literature of the area. It is said that he became familiar with every ruin and every battleground in the region.

Scott, after turning his back on law to pursue a literary career, became known as a collector of ballads. His first literary success, *Minstrelsy of the Scottish Border*, was published in 1802. This book was one of the first collections of traditional ballads many of which related the tales of the Border country Scott had heard as a boy. Most of these ballads were published for the first time in this book, and hence Scott is credited with preserving, for future generations, a wealth of traditional ballads that might otherwise have been lost.

Scott also translated some German ballads and composed ballads of his own imitating the traditional ballad form he had learned. "Lochinvar" is one well-known example of Scott's ballads.

Scott is better known for his metrical romances. These are long complex narrative poems of which "Lady of the Lake" is an example. This one-hundred-page poem, composed in 1809, is considered one of the best metrical romances in English literature. Scott was also well known for his criticism and review.

Scott's greatest success came as a writer of popular historical romance. He wrote nearly thirty of these novels in his lifetime. *Ivanhoe* is one of his novels that is still widely read today.

At the height of his career, Sir Walter Scott was the most renowned writer of his day. He enjoyed tremendous popularity all through Europe and in the United States. Through his works, Scott presented his country, its people and its history, to the world. He became a national hero.

Writing brought Scott wealth as well as great renown. He was able to live a comfortable life on his estate at Abbotsford for many years. He is known to have worked on his writing in the morning before his family awoke. His afternoons were taken up with his family, with riding and hunting. In 1825, during a serious economic depression in England, Scott was financially ruined. He wrote feverishly to pay his debts and repaid most of them before his death in 1832. In spite of his financial failure, Scott retained his good humour and dignity to the end.

Hunting Song

Waken, lords and ladies gay!
On the mountain dawns the day,
All the jolly chase is here,
With hawk, and horse, and hunting-spear;
Hounds are in their couples yelling,
Hawks are whistling, horns are knelling,
Merrily, merrily, mingle they,
"Waken, lords and ladies gay."

Waken, lords and ladies gay!
The mist has left the mountain gray,
Springlets in the dawn are steaming,
Diamonds on the brake are gleaming;
And foresters have busy been
To track the buck in thicket green;
Now we come to chant our lay,
"Waken, lords and ladies gay."

Waken, lords and ladies gay!
To the green-wood haste away;
We can show you where he lies,
Fleet of foot, and tall of size;
We can show the marks he made,
When 'gainst the oak his antlers frayed;
You shall see him brought to bay, —
"Waken, lords and ladies gay."

Louder, louder chant the lay,
Waken, lords and ladies gay!
Tell them youth, and mirth, and glee,
Run a course as well as we;
Time, stern huntsman! who can balk,
Stanch as hound, and fleet as hawk?
Think of this, and rise with day,
Gentle lords and ladies gay.

Border March

March, march, Ettrick and Teviotdale,
  Why the deil dinna ye march forward in order?
March, march, Eskdale and Liddesdale,
  All the Blue Bonnets are bound for the Border.
    Many a banner spread,
    Flutters above your head,
  Many a crest that is famous in story.
    Mount and make ready then,
    Sons of the mountain glen,
  Fight for the Queen and our old Scottish glory.

II

Come from the hills where your hirsels are grazing,
  Come from the glen of the buck and the roe;
Come to the crag where the beacon is blazing,
  Come with the buckler, the lance, and the bow.
    Trumpets are sounding,
    War-steeds are bounding,
  Stand to your arms and march in good order,
    England shall many a day
    Tell of the bloody fray,
  When the Blue Bonnets came over the Border.

Bonny Dundee

To the Lords of Convention 'twas
    Claver'se who spoke,
'Ere the King's crown shall fall there
    are crowns to be broke;
So let each Cavalier who loves honour
    and me,
Come follow the bonnet of Bonny
    Dundee.

Chorus:
    'Come fill up my cup, come fill up
        my can,
    Come saddle your horses, and call
        up your men;
    Come open the West Port, and let
        me gang free,
    And it's room for the bonnets of
        Bonny Dundee!'

Dundee he is mounted, he rides up
    the street,
The bells are rung backward, the
    drums they are beat;
But the Provost, douce man, said,
    'Just e'en let him be,
The Gude Town is weel quit of that
    Deil of Dundee.

    Come fill up my cup, &c.

As he rode down the sanctified bends
    of the Bow,
Ilk carline was flyting and shaking her
    pow;
But the young plants of grace they
    look'd couthie and slee,
Thinking, 'Luck to thy bonnet, thou
    Bonny Dundee!'

    Come fill up my cup, &c.

With sour-featured Whigs the Grass-
    market was cramm'd
As if half the West had set tryst to
    be hang'd;
There was spite in each look, there
    was fear in each e'e,

As they watch'd for the bonnets of
    Bonny Dundee.

    Come fill up my cup, &c.

These cowls of Kilmarnock had spits
    and had spears,
And lang-hafted gullies to kill Cavaliers;
But they shrunk to close-heads, and
    the causeway was free,
At the toss of the bonnet of Bonny
    Dundee.

    Come fill up my cup, &c.

He spurr'd to the foot of the proud
    Castle rock,
And with the gay Gordon he gallantly
    spoke;
'Let Mons Meg and her marrows
    speak twa words or three,
For the love of the bonnet of Bonny
    Dundee.'

    Come fill up my cup, &c.

The Gordon demands of him which
    way he goes —
'Where'er shall direct me the shade
    of Montrose!
Your Grace in short space shall hear
    tidings of me,
Or that low lies the bonnet of Bonny
    Dundee.

    Come fill up my cup, &c.

'There are hills beyond Pentland, and
    lands beyond Forth,
If there's lords in the Lowlands,
    there's chiefs in the North;
There are wild Duniewassals, three
    thousand times three,
Will cry *hoigh!* for the bonnet of
    Bonny Dundee.

    Come fill up my cup, &c.

'There's brass on the target of
    barken'd bull-hide;
There's steel in the scabbard that
    dangles beside;
The brass shall be burnish'd, the steel
    shall flash free,
At a toss of the bonnet of Bonny
    Dundee.

    Come fill up my cup, &c.

'Away to the hills, to the caves, to
    the rocks —
Ere I own an usurper, I'll couch with
    the fox;
And tremble, false Whigs, in the
    midst of your glee,
You have not seen the last of my
    bonnet and me!'

Come fill up my cup, &c.

He waved his proud hand, and the
    trumpets were blown,
The kettle-drums clash'd, and the
    horsemen rode on,
Till on Ravelston's cliffs and on
    Clermiston's lee,
Died away the wild war-notes of
    Bonny Dundee.

    Come fill up my cup, come fill up
      my can,
    Come saddle the horses and call up
      the men,
    Come open your gates, and let me
      gae free,
    For it's up with the bonnets of
      Bonny Dundee!

Focus on Sir Walter Scott

1. Scott was a romantic, proud of his Scottish heritage and history. Make a list of words and phrases used in the poems in this collection which reveal Scott's sense of pride.

2. Organize a "Sir Walter Scott Day" for your class or for your school. Become involved in one or more of the following activities that could be presented to the class or other classes.
   * recitals of traditional Border ballads
   * recitals of Scott's shorter poems
   * a dramatization of one scene from one of Scott's ballads
   * a folk concert of traditional Border ballads
   * an oral presentation on one of Scott's metrical romances
   * an oral presentation on one of Scott's novels
   * a book display of Scott's works

3. Much of Scott's writing is based, at least in part, on historical fact. Research the wars between England and Scotland and the history of the Border country. Select one incident or one battle in this long struggle and write a one-page summary of it.

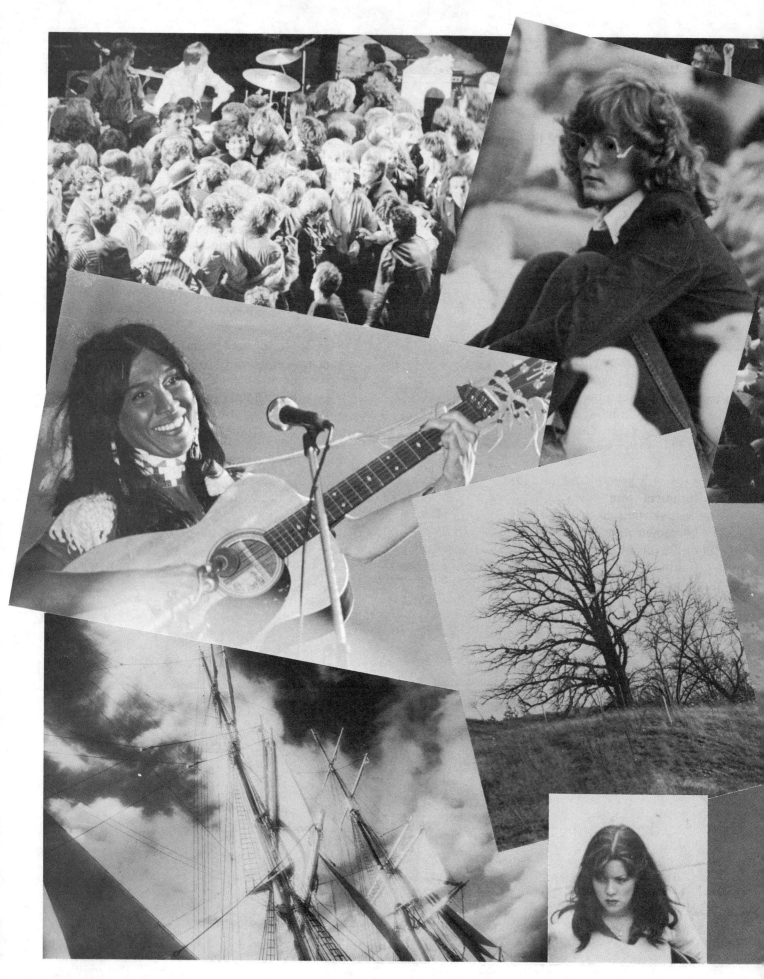

Literary Tales in Ballad Form

The literary ballad has its roots in the traditional ballad, sharing many characteristics with this earlier form. The literary ballad is different in that it is composed by a person who considers himself or herself to be a poet. Poets such as Keats, Tennyson, Auden, Longfellow, Sandburg, and Noyes are well known for their literary ballads. Being more artistic than the traditional ballad, the literary ballad is also known as the art ballad. Literary ballads are carefully planned, highly polished, contain more detail than the traditional ballad, and use carefully chosen literary devices. They are not usually composed to be sung. While being more "poetic," literary ballads lack the stark realism and simplicity of the original form.

In recent years, a modern form of literary ballad called the modern folk song has gained in popularity. These modern ballads are often simpler than the earlier literary ballads and have become popular as songs. During the Depression of the thirties, the legendary Woodie Guthrie was in the forefront of a new group of composers whose songs commented on the social issues of the day. During the fifties, groups such as The Weavers, The Kingston Trio, The Chad Mitchell Trio, The Travellers, and The Brothers Four were popular as performers of both traditional and modern ballads. In the early sixties, folk ballads again became very popular. This new generation of literary ballads commented strongly on social justice issues related especially to civil rights, the peace movement, and environmental concerns. Some of the best known of the modern balladeers are Bob Dylan, Gordon Lightfoot, Judy Collins, Pete Seeger, Phil Ochs, Ian Tyson, Buffy Saint-Marie, Harry Chapin, Chris de Burg, and Roger Whittaker.

All of the poems in this unit are literary ballads. Some have more literary merit than others, yet they all have a story to tell. As you read or listen to the following ballads, notice how the simple story is enriched by the literary skills of the poet.

The story of Robin Hood is familiar to many. As you may recall in this story, the leader of a band of thieves and his followers are considered to be the heroes. Though Robin and his band live outside the law, they are "heroes" because they take from the evil, unjust rich and give to the needy, downtrodden poor. The villains of the story are the protectors of established law and order, the Sheriff of Nottingham and his force. These early "police officers" are seen as the villains in this famous story because the existing social order which they police is described as corrupt and unjust. Is Robin Hood an outlaw or a hero? It all depends on point of view — on the side one supports.

The main characters in the ballads in this chapter are gallant heroes or common outlaws, depending on one's point of view. All defy the established authority of the time. As you read these poems, try to develop your own point of view. Are these people heroes, outlaws, or something else?

Heather Ale
Robert Louis Stevenson

From the bonny bells of heather
　　They brewed a drink long-syne,
Was sweeter far than honey,
　　Was stronger far than wine.
They brewed it and they drank it,
　　And lay in a blessed swound
For days and days together
　　In their dwellings underground.

There rose a king in Scotland,
　　A fell man to his foes,
He smote the Picts in battle,
　　He hunted them like roes.
Over miles of the red mountain
　　He hunted as they fled,
And strewed the dwarfish bodies
　　Of the dying and the dead.

Summer came in the country,
　　Red was the heather bell;
But the manner of the brewing
　　Was none alive to tell.
In graves that were like children's
　　On many a mountain head,
The Brewsters of the Heather
　　Lay numbered with the dead.

The king in the red moorland
　　Rode on a summer's day;
And the bees hummed, and the curlews
　　Cried beside the way.
The king rode, and was angry,
　　Black was his brow and pale,
To rule in a land of heather
　　And lack the Heather Ale.

It fortuned that his vassals,
　　Riding free on the heath,
Came on a stone that was fallen
　　And vermin hid beneath.
Rudely plucked from their hiding,
　　Never a word they spoke:
A son and his aged father —
　　Last of the dwarfish folk.

The king sat high on his charger,
  He looked on the little men;
And the dwarfish and swarthy couple
  Looked at the king again.
Down by the shore he had them;
  And there on the giddy brink —
'I will give you life, ye vermin,
  For the secret of the drink.'

There stood the son and father
  And they looked high and low;
The heather was red around them
  The sea rumbled below.
And up and spoke the father,
  Shrill was his voice to hear:
'I have a word in private,
  A word for the royal ear.

'Life is dear to the aged,
  And honour a little thing;
I would glady sell the secret,'
  Quoth the Pict to the King.
His voice was small as a sparrow's,
  And shrill and wonderful clear;
'I would gladly sell my secret,
  Only my son I fear.

'For life is a little matter,
  And death is nought to the young;
And I dare not sell my honour
  Under the eye of my son.
Take *him*, O king, and bind him,
  And cast him far in the deep;
And it's I will tell the secret
  That I have sworn to keep.'

They took the son and bound him,
  Neck and heels in a thong,
And a lad took him and swung him,
  And flung him far and strong,
And the sea swallowed his body,
  Like that of a child of ten; —
And there on the cliff stood the father,
  Last of the dwarfish men.

'True was the word I told you;
  Only my son I feared;
For I doubt the sapling courage
  That goes without the beard.
But now in vain is the torture,
  Fire shall never avail:
Here dies in my bosom
  The secret of Heather Ale.'

Waltzing Matilda

A.B. Paterson

Once a jolly swagman camped by a billabong
Under the shade of a coolibah tree,
And he sang as he watched and waited till his billy boiled,
"You'll come a-waltzing Matilda with me!"

Chorus:
Waltzing Matilda, Waltzing Matilda,
You'll come a-waltzing Matilda with me.
And he sang as he watched and waited till his billy boiled.
            (stowed that jum-buck in his tucker bag)
"You'll come a-waltzing Matilda with me!"

Down came a jumbuck to drink at the billabong,
Up jumped the swagman and grabbed him with glee,
And he sang as he stowed that jum-buck in his tucker bag,
"You'll come a-waltzing Matilda with me!"

Up rode the squatter, mounted on his thoroughbred,
Down came the troopers, one, two three:
"Where's that jolly jumbuck
You've got in your tucker bag?"
"You'll come a-waltzing Matilda with me!"

Up jumped the swagman, sprang into the billabong.
"You'll never catch me alive," said he.
And his ghost may be heard as you pass by that billabong,
"You'll come a-waltzing Matilda with me!"

The Highwayman

Alfred Noyes

Part 1

1 The wind was a torrent of darkness among the gusty trees,
The moon was a ghostly galleon tossed upon cloudy seas,
The road was a ribbon of moonlight over the purple moor,
And the highwayman came riding —
　　　Riding — riding —
The highwayman came riding, up to the old inn-door.

He'd a French cocked-hat on his forehead, a bunch of lace at his chin,
A coat of the claret velvet, and breeches of brown doeskin:
They fitted with never a wrinkle; his boots were up to the thigh!
And he rode with a jewelled twinkle,
　　　His pistol butts a-twinkle,
His rapier hilt a-twinkle, under the jewelled sky.

3 Over the cobbles he clattered and clashed in the dark inn-yard,
And he tapped with his whip on the shutters, but all was locked and barred:
He whistled a tune to the window, and who should be waiting there
But the landlord's black-eyed daughter,
　　　Bess, the landlord's daughter,
Plaiting a dark red love-knot into her long black hair.

4 And dark in the dark old inn-yard a stable-wicket creaked
Where Tim, the ostler, listened; his face was white and peaked.
His eyes were hollows of madness, his hair like moldy hay;
But he loved the landlord's daughter,
　　　The landlord's red-lipped daughter:
Dumb as a dog he listened, and he heard the robber say —

5 "One kiss, my bonny sweetheart, I'm after a prize tonight,
But I shall be back with the yellow gold before the morning light.
Yet if they press me sharply, and harry me through the day,
Then look for me by moonlight,
　　　Watch for me by moonlight:
I'll come to thee by moonlight, though Hell should bar the way."

6 He rose upright in the stirrups, he scarce could reach her hand;
But she loosened her hair i' the casement! His face burnt like a brand
As the black cascade of perfume came tumbling over his breast;
And he kissed its waves in the moonlight,
　　　(Oh, sweet black waves in the moonlight)
Then he tugged at his reins in the moonlight, and galloped away to the
　　　West.

Part 2

He did not come in the dawning; he did not come at noon;
And out of the tawny sunset, before the rise o' the moon,
When the road was a gypsy's ribbon, looping the purple moor,
A red-coat troop came marching —
        Marching — marching —
King George's men came marching, up to the old inn-door.

They said no word to the landlord, they drank his ale instead;
But they gagged his daughter and bound her to the foot of her narrow bed.
Two of them knelt at her casement, with muskets at their side!
There was death at every window;
        And Hell at one dark window;
For Bess could see, through her casement, the road that *he* would ride.

They had tied her up to attention, with many a sniggering jest:
They had bound a musket beside her, with the barrel beneath her
        breast!
"Now keep good watch!" and they kissed her.
        She heard the dead man say —
Look for me by moonlight;
        Watch for me by moonlight;
I'll come to thee by moonlight, though Hell should bar the way!

She twisted her hands behind her; but all the knots held good!
She writhed her hands till her fingers were wet with sweat or blood!
They stretched and strained in the darkness, and the hours crawled by like
        years;
Till, now, on the stroke of midnight,
        Cold, on the stroke of midnight,
The tip of one finger touched it! The trigger at least was hers!

The tip of one finger touched it; she strove no more for the rest!
Up, she stood up to attention, with the barrel beneath her breast,
She would not risk their hearing: she would not strive again;
For the road lay bare in the moonlight,
        Blank and bare in the moonlight;
And the blood of her veins in the moonlight throbbed to her Love's refrain.

Tlot-tlot, tlot-tlot! Had they heard it? The horse-hoofs ringing clear —
Tlot-tlot, tlot-tlot, in the distance? Were they deaf that they did not hear?
Down the ribbon of moonlight, over the brow of the hill,
The highwayman came riding,
        Riding, riding!
The red-coats looked to their priming! She stood up straight and still!

12 *Tlot-tlot*, in the frosty silence! *Tlot-tlot* in the echoing night!
Nearer he came and nearer! Her face was like a light!
Her eyes grew wide for a moment; she drew one last deep breath,
Then her finger moved in the moonlight,
 Her musket shattered the moonlight,
Shattered her breast in the moonlight and warned him — with her death.

14 He turned; he spurred to the Westward; he did not know who stood
Bowed with her head o'er the musket, drenched with her own red blood!
Not till the dawn he heard it, and slowly blanched to hear
How Bess, the landlord's daughter,
 The landlord's black-eyed daughter,
Had watched for her Love in the moonlight; and died in the darkness
 there.

15 Back, he spurred like a madman, shrieking a curse to the sky,
With the white road smoking behind him, and his rapier brandished high!
Blood-red were his spurs i' the golden noon; wine-red was his velvet coat;
When they shot him down on the highway,
 Down like a dog on the highway,
And he lay in his blood on the highway, with a bunch of lace at his throat.

16 *And still of a winter's night, they say, when the wind is in the trees,*
When the moon is a ghostly galleon tossed upon cloudy seas,
When the road is a ribbon of moonlight over the purple moor,
A highwayman comes riding —
 Riding — riding —
A highwayman comes riding, up to the old inn-door.

Over the cobbles he clatters and clangs in the dark inn-yard;
And he taps with his whip on the shutters, but all is locked and barred:
He whistles a tune to the window, and who should be waiting there
But the landlord's black-eyed daughter,
 Bess, the landlord's daughter,
Plaiting a dark red love-knot into her long black hair.

1. How do the heroes in each poem defy established authority?

2. What forces are in conflict in each poem? How was the conflict in each resolved?

3. Write a descriptive paragraph. Use one of the major characters from one of the poems in this chapter as your subject. Use details from the poem. Remember that your task is to describe one of these subjects and not to narrate.

4. With a small group, select one of the poems from this chapter and prepare to read it aloud. Plan your interpretation and your arrangement of the parts in the poem. Rehearse your presentation. Add sound effects, if you like. Play a tape recording of your poem or present it live to the class. Compare your arrangement with that of another group which selected the same poem.

5. All of the main characters in these poems are outlaws yet they are presented as heroes. List modern 'good guys' from television or the movies that usually find themselves on the other side of the law. Would you consider them heroes? Why or why not?

6. Hold a debate around one of the following resolutions:
   - The highwayman was nothing more than a common thief.
   - It was not worth dying to keep the secret of Heather Ale.

7. Dramatize "The Highwayman" in the form of a radio play. You will need an announcer, a narrator, and actors. You may want to use a chorus, music, and sound effects. It will be necessary to write a script and to rehearse your drama. Tape your radio play or do it live for the class.

10 Towards a Better World

Bob Dylan, one of the most influential folk poets of the early sixties tells us, "And the times, they are a'changin'." The twentieth century has been one of great transition. In 1900 many travelled by horse and buggy. In 1982 we have flown spaceships into space and brought them back again. Change has become a central theme in literature. While we are aware of rapid change, we more and more want to influence the direction of change. Society today is more aware, more knowledgeable, and more outspoken about change. It is more committed to having some influence over change. If we don't like what we see in society, we are better prepared to speak out or to make protest to effect changes we believe to be desirable.

Although particularly alive in the early sixties, protest movements have always been with us and always will be. The tradition of protest is not new. During the Middle Ages, university students were outspoken protestors of the existing social order. Protestantism has, as its root, the word *protest*. Blake and Shelley were writers of protest poetry in their day. They were both appalled and outraged by war and would have been in the forefront of the Peace Marches of the sixties. William Butler Yeats was an ardent protestor of the evils in society. Like the modern American folk poet, Phil Ochs, Yeats became a predictor of doom for a society that was beyond saving. Walt Whitman, an outspoken critic of conventionalism, and Henry David Thoreau, who protested materialism, had much in common with the "flower power" generation and would have felt quite at home at Woodstock. Poets have always been protestors. They have always worked towards a better world.

As a reader of protest poetry one does not necessarily have to believe in the point of view being presented to enjoy the poem. Reading a poem which cries out against the horrors of war can help us experience what the poet is describing, and share the feelings evoked. To enjoy and appreciate the poem does not mean that we must also wholeheartedly embrace the ideas being presented.

Some literary ballads are written to comment on some believed truth about life or to persuade the listener of the justice of some moral point of view. In recent times, these ballads have often taken the form of the folk song. Such songs were most popular during the Great Depression and again during the sixties. These song poems comment on topics such as war, civil rights, poverty, unionism, alienation, injustice, and ecology. Some of the most successful writers of this form of literary ballad are Woodie Guthrie, Bob Dylan, Pete Seeger, Judy Collins, Phil Ochs, John Prine, Buffy St. Marie, Paul Simon, Neil Young, Joni Mitchell, and Harry Chapin. As you study the song poems with a message in this chapter, decide whether you agree or disagree with the points of view put forward. Seek out other examples of this form composed by the writers listed above and discuss the social-justice statements made.

Cats in the Cradle
Harry and Sandy Chapin

A child arrived just the other day.
He came into the world in the usual way.
But there were planes to catch and bills to pay.
He learned to walk while I was away.
And he was talking 'fore I knew it
And as he grew he'd say,
"I'm gonna be like you, Dad.
You know I'm gonna be like you."

And the cats in the cradle,
and the silver spoon
Little Boy Blue
And the Man in the Moon.
"When you comin' home, Dad?
"I don't know when, but we'll get together then, son.
You know we'll have a good time then."

Well, my son turned ten, just the other day.
He said, "Thanks for the ball, Dad.
Come on, let's play.
Can you teach me to throw?"
I said, "Not today. I've got a lot to do."
He said, "That's okay."
And he walked away, but his smile never dimmed.
And he said, "I'm gonna be like him.
You know I'm gonna be like him."

And the cats in the cradle,
and the silver spoon,
Little Boy Blue
And the Man in the Moon.
"When you comin' home, Dad?"
"I don't know when, but we'll get together then,
  son.
You know we'll have a good time then."

Well, he came from college just the other day,
So much like a man I just had to say,
"Son, I'm proud of you.
Can you sit for a while?"
He shook his head
And he said with a smile,
"What I'd really like, Dad, is to borrow the car
  keys.
See you later.
Can I have them, please?"

And the cats in the cradle,
and the silver spoon,
Little Boy Blue
And the Man in the Moon.
"When you comin' home, son?"
"I don't know when, but we'll get together then,
  Dad.
You know we'll have a good time then."

Well, I've long since retired.
My son's moved away.
I called him up just the other day.
I said, "I'd like to see you, if you don't mind."
He said, "I'd love to, Dad, if I can find the time
You see, my new job's a hassle and the kids have
  the flu.
But it's sure nice talking to you, Dad.
It's been sure nice talking to you."
And as he hung up the phone, it occurred to me
He had grown up just like me.
My boy was just like me.

And the cats in the cradle,
and the silver spoon,
Little Boy Blue
And the Man in the Moon.
"When you comin' home, son?"
"I don't know when, but we'll get together then,
  Dad.
You know we'll have a good time then."

Ballad of Birmingham
Dudley Randall

Mother dear may I go downtown
Instead of out to play
and march the streets of Birmingham
In a freedom march today?

No baby no, you may not go
For the dogs are fierce and wild,
And clubs and hoses, guns and jails
Aren't for a little child.

But mother I won't be alone,
Other children will go with me
And march the streets of Birmingham
To make our people free.

No baby no, you may not go
I fear the guns will fire,
But you may go to church instead and sing in the
  children's choir.

She's combed and brushed her night dark hair
And bathed rose petal sweet,
And drawn white gloves on small brown hands,
White shoes on her feet.

Her mother smiled to know her child
Was in that sacred place,
But that smile was the last
Smile to come to her face.

For when she heard the explosion
Her eyes grew wet and wild,
She raced through the streets of Birmingham
Yelling for her child.

She dug in bits of glass and brick,
Then pulled out a shoe —
O here is the shoe my baby wore
But baby where are you?

The Universal Soldier
Buffy Sainte-Marie

He's five foot two and he's six feet four,
   he fights with missiles and with spears,
He's all of thirty-one and he's only seventeen,
   he's been a soldier for a thousand years.

He's a Catholic, a Hindu, an Atheist, a Jain,
   a Buddhist and a Baptist and a Jew,
And he knows he shouldn't kill and he knows he always will
   kill you for me, my friend, and me for you;

And he's fighting for Canada, he's fighting for France,
   he's fighting for the U.S.A.,
And he's fighting for the Russians and he's fighting for Japan,
   and he thinks we'll put an end to war that way.

And he's fighting for democracy, he's fighting for the Reds,
   he says it's for the peace of all,
He's the one who must decide who's to live and who's to die,
   and he never sees the writing on the wall.

But without him how would Hitler have condemned him at Dachau,
   without him Caesar would have stood alone,
He's the one who gives his body as a weapon of the war,
   and without him all this killing can't go on.

He's the Universal Soldier and he really is to blame,
   his orders come from far away no more,
They come from him and you and me, and, brothers can't you see,
   This is not the way we put an end to war.

The Times They Are A-Changin'
Bob Dylan

Come gather 'round people
Wherever you roam
And admit that the waters
Around you have grown
And accept it that soon
You'll be drenched to the bone,
If your time to you
Is worth savin'
Then you better start swimmin'
Or you'll sink like a stone,
For the times they are a-changin'!

Come writers and critics
Who prophesy with your pen
And keep your eyes wide
The chance won't come again.
And don't speak too soon
For the wheel's still in spin
And there's no tellin' who
That it's namin'
For the loser now
Will be later to win
For the times they are a-changin'.

Come senators, congressmen
Please heed the call
Don't stand in the doorway
Don't block up the hall.
For he that gets hurt
Will be he who has stalled
There's a battle
Outside and it's ragin'
It'll soon shake your windows
And rattle your walls
For the times they are a-changin'.

Come mothers and fathers,
Throughout the land
And don't criticize
What you can't understand.
Your sons and your daughters
Are beyond your command
Your old road is
Rapidly agin'
Please get out of the new one
If you can't lend your hand
For the times they are a-changin'.

The line it is drawn
The curse it is cast
The slow one now will
Later be fast.
As the present now
Will later be past
The order is rapidly fadin'
And the first one now
Will later be last
For the times they are a-changin'.

Focus on Meaning

1. Make a collection of poems on the theme of war. Some poems to look for might be:
"Dulce Et Decorum Est" — Wilfred Owen
"I Ain't Marching Anymore" — Phil Ochs
"The Battle of Blenheim" — Robert Southey
"The Man He Killed" — Thomas Hardy
"In Flanders Fields" — John McCrae
"The Charge of the Light Brigade" — Alfred Lord Tennyson
Some of these poems celebrate past glories while others comment strongly against war. Many points of view may be represented in your collection. Write a one-page paper on the theme of war in poetry based on the poems you have gathered.

2. Select one poet referred to in this chapter and do a detailed study of his or her life and works. Refer to anthologies, records, biographies, and other sources to collect your information. Prepare a written or oral report that:
   • deals with the life of the poet
   • comments on his or her major poems with regard to theme

3. Many song poems in the sixties commented on the American civil rights movement and later on the peace movement. Listen to a variety of song poems recorded by such singers as Joni Mitchell, Phil Ochs, Joan Baez, Paul Simon, Judy Collins, and Peter, Paul and Mary that deal with one of these issues. Prepare an oral report on the movement you selected to study as it was recorded in these song poems. Newspaper articles from the period and other resources could be used to support your presentation.

4. Harry Chapin was well known during the seventies as a singer/composer of what he called story songs. All of Chapin's song poems tell a detailed story and at the same time attempt to point out to us some truth about life. Study several of Chapin's story songs and prepare an oral report for the class that focusses on the messages he presents to his listeners.

5. Buffy Sainte-Marie, Paul Simon, and Bob Dylan have had their song poems recorded by numerous singers. Research records in your own collection or in record stores and make as complete a list as possible of the various artists that have recorded their songs. List the artist with the song recorded. Note how many different singers have recorded these writers' most popular song poems. Make a brief report to the class on your findings.

6. Organize an evening of folk singing and poetry reading for your school. Set up a section of your gymnasium as a coffee house with tables, chairs, and a small stage at the front. Individuals can take turns singing or reading story poems that make some social comment. You may invite a local folksinger to perform. You may wish to serve coffee, soft drinks, and snacks at your "coffee house."

11 The Cruel Sea

Seafarers throughout history have been married to the sea and this bond between seafarer and sea is many faceted. It is a love-hate relationship. The sea as provider is described in loving terms. It is the parent that generously gives so that the seafarer can enjoy the pleasures of home and family. The sea as destroyer is described in violent terms. It is the hungry dog or raging devil that attacks ships and batters them against reefs and rocky shores. Seafarers have always had to respect the great power of the sea to bring home a good catch, to deliver an important cargo, or to transport travellers.

Even in modern times, those who fish or sail for a living face many hazards when they go to sea. Modern technology has made the sea a safer place on which to work but from time to time even the most sophisticated of ships and oil rigs fall victim to the power of the sea. In spite of these risks many men and women in Atlantic Canada, British Columbia, and the Great Lakes region make fishing and sailoring a way of life.

The awesome power of the sea and its effect on humanity has made it a popular theme in literature. Great and perilous sea voyages were often major components of Greek and Roman myths. Numerous other stories and poems have been composed since these that attempt to capture this daring, rugged lifestyle. In Canada we have a rich heritage of sea ballads that recount distressing tales of brave sailors, bold captains, powerful gales, and spectacular shipwrecks.

All of the poems in this chapter tell the tale of a ship lost at sea. Two of these accounts are based on true stories. As you read or listen to these poems, try to develop an appreciation of the seafarer's unique way of life.

The Wreck of the Hesperus
Henry Wadsworth Longfellow

It was the schooner Hesperus,
    That sailed the wintry sea;
And the skipper had taken his little daughtèr,
    To bear him company.

Blue were her eyes as the fairy-flax,
    Her cheeks like the dawn of the day,
And her bosom white as the hawthorn buds,
    That ope in the month of May.

The skipper he stood beside the helm,
    His pipe was in his mouth,
And he watched how the veering flaw did blow
    The smoke now West, now South.

Then up and spake an old Sailòr,
    Had sailed to the Spanish Main,
"I pray thee, put into yonder port,
    For I fear a hurricane.

"Last night, the moon had a golden ring,
    And to-night no moon we see!"
The skipper, he blew a whiff from his pipe,
    And a scornful laugh laughed he.

Colder and louder blew the wind,
    A gale from the Northeast,
The snow fell hissing in the brine,
    And the billows frothed like yeast.

Down came the storm, and smote again
    The vessel in its strength;
She shuddered and paused, like a frighted steed,
    Then leaped her cable's length.

"Come hither! come hither! my little daughtèr,
    And do not tremble so;
For I can weather the roughest gale
    That ever wind did blow."

He wrapped her warm in his seaman's coat
    Against the stinging blast;
He cut a rope from a broken spar,
    And bound her to the mast.

"O father! I hear the church-bells ring,
　　Oh say, what may it be?"
"'Tis a fog-bell on a rock-bound coast!"
　　And he steered for the open sea.

"O father! I hear the sound of guns,
　　Oh say, what may it be?"
"Some ship in distress, that cannot live
　　In such an angry sea!"

"O father! I see a gleaming light,
　　Oh say, what may it be?"
But the father answered never a word,
　　A frozen corpse was he.

Lashed to the helm, all stiff and stark,
　　With his face turned to the skies,
The lantern gleamed through the gleaming snow
　　On his fixed and glassy eyes.

Then the maiden clasped her hands and prayed
　　That saved she might be;
And she thought of Christ, who stilled the wave,
　　On the lake of Galilee.

And fast through the midnight dark and drear,
　　Through the whistling sleet and snow,
Like a sheeted ghost, the vessel swept
　　Tow'rds the reef of Norman's Woe.

And ever the fitful gusts between
　　A sound came from the land;
It was the sound of the trampling surf
　　On the rocks and the hard sea-sand.

The breakers were right beneath her bows,
　　She drifted a dreary wreck,
And a whooping billow swept the crew
　　Like icicles from her deck.

She struck where the white and fleecy waves
　　Looked soft as carded wool,
But the cruel rocks, they gored her side
　　Like the horns of an angry bull.

Her rattling shrouds, all sheathed in ice,
　　With the masts went by the board;
Like a vessel of glass, she stove and sank,
　　Ho! ho! the breakers roared!

At daybreak, on a bleak sea-beach,
　　A fisherman stood aghast,
To see the form of a maiden fair,
　　Lashed close to a drifting mast.

The salt sea was frozen on her breast,
　　The salt tears in her eyes;
And he saw her hair, like the brown sea-weed,
　　On the billows fall and rise.

Such was the wreck of the Hesperus,
　　In the midnight and the snow!
Christ save us all from a death like this,
　　On the reef of Norman's Woe.

The Wreck of the Edmund Fitzgerald
Gordon Lightfoot

The legend lives on from the Chippewa on down of the big lake
    they called Gitche Gumee.
The lake it is said never gives up her dead, when the skies of
    November turn gloomy.
With a load of iron ore 26,000 tons more than the Edmund Fitzgerald
    weighed empty
That good ship and true was a bone to be chewed when the gales of
    November came early.

The ship was the pride of the American side, comin' back from some
    mill in Wisconsin.
As the big freighters go it was bigger than most, with a crew
    and good captain well seasoned,
Concluding some terms with a couple of steel firms, when they
    left fully loaded for Cleveland,
And later that night when the ship's bell rang, could it be the
    north wind they's bin feelin'.

The wind in the wires made a tattletale sound and a wave broke over
    the railing,
And every man knew as the captain did too, 'twas the witch of
    November come stealin'.
The dawn came late and the breakfast had to wait, when the gales
    of November came slashin'.
When afternoon came it was freezin' rain, in the face of a hurricane
    west wind.

When suppertime came the old cook came on deck saying, "Fellas
    it's too rough to feed ya."
At seven p.m. a main hatchway caved in he said, "Fellas it's bin
    good to know ya."
The captain wired in he had water comin' in and the good ship and
    crew was in peril,
And later that night when its lights went out of sight came the
    wreck of the Edmund Fitzgerald.

Does anyone know where the love of God goes when the waves turn
    the minutes to hours?
The searchers all say they'd have made Whitefish Bay — if they'd
    put fifteen more miles behind 'em.
They might have split up or they might have capsized, they may have
    broke deep and took water,
And all that remains is the faces and the names of the wives and
    the sons and the daughters.

Lake Huron rolls, Superior sings, in the rooms of her ice water
   mansion,
Old Michigan steams like a young man's dreams, the islands and
   bays are for sportsmen,
And farther below Lake Ontario takes in what Lake Erie can send
   her,
And the Iron boats go as the mariners all know, with the gales
   of November remembered.

In a musty old hall in Detroit they prayed in the maritime
   sailors' cathedral,
The church bell chimed 'til it rang 29 times for each man on
   the Edmund Fitzgerald.
The legend lives on from the Chippewa on down of the big lake
   they called Gitche Gumee.
Superior they said never gives up her dead when the gales of
   November come early.

The Ballad of the Bluenose
David Martins

In the town of Lunenburg down Nova Scotia way,
In nineteen twenty-one on a windy day,
A sailing ship was born — the Bluenose was her name,
You'll never see her kind again.

Refrain: Bluenose! The ocean knows her name,
            Sailors know how proud a ship was she.
            Bluenose! Leaning in the wind,
            Racing ev'ry wave on the sea.

Her sails were snowy white, they strained against the mast,
Her spray flew high as she went racing past,
And from the very first, the Bluenose loved to run,
She loved the smell of sea and of sun.

For twenty-five long years she ruled the Northern sea,
Riding like a queen on the tide,
But in the Caribbean one dark and stormy day,
She ran into a reef and died.

Now just the other day, down Nova Scotia way,
In Lunenburg they christened a ship,
Just like the old Bluenose down to the very name,
The Bluenose lives and sails again.

The Wreck of the "Julie Plante"
William Henry Drummond

On wan dark night on Lac St. Pierre,
   De win' she blow, blow, blow,
An' de crew of de wood scow "Julie Plante"
   Got scar't an' run below —
For de win' she blow lak' hurricane
   Bimeby she blow some more,
An' de scow bus' up on Lac St. Pierre
   Wan arpent from de shore.

De captinne walk on de fronte deck,
   An' walk de hin' deck too —
He call de crew from up de hole
   He call de cook also.
De cook she's name was Rosie,
   She come from Montreal,
Was chambre maid on lumber barge,
   On de Grande Lachine Canal.

De win' she blow from nor'/eas'/wes' —
   De sout' win' she blow too,
W'en Rosie cry "Mon cher captinne,
   Mon cher, w'at I shall do?"
Den de captinne t'row de big ankerre,
   But still the scow she dreef',
De crew he can't pass on de shore,
   Becos' he los' hees skeef.

De night was dark lak' wan black cat,
   De wave run high an' fas',
W'en de captinne tak' de Rosie girl
   An' tie her to de mas'.
Den he also tak' de life preserve,
   An' jomp off on de lak',
An' say, "Good-bye, ma Rosie dear,
   I go drown for your sak'."

Nex' morning very early
   'Bout ha'f-pas' two — t'ree — four —
De captinne — scow — an' de poor Rosie
   Was corpses on de shore,
For de win' she blow lak' hurricane
   Bimeby she blow some more,
An' de scow bus' up on Lac St. Pierre,
   Wan arpent from de shore.

Moral

Now all good wood scow sailor man
   Tak' warning by dat storm
An' go an' marry some nice French girl
   An' leev on wan beeg farm.
De win' can blow lak' hurricane
   An' s'pose she blow some more,
You can't get drown on Lac St. Pierre
   So long you stay on shore.

Focus on Meaning

1. Memorize "The Wreck of the Hesperus" or "The Wreck of the "Julie Plante'" and prepare it for recitation. In groups of four, take turns reciting your poems. You may want to present your interpretation of your poem to the class.

2. The freighter *Edmund Fitzgerald* did sink in Lake Superior on a stormy November day in 1975 with the loss of all hands. Like many ballads, the Lightfoot account of this tragedy is based on historical fact. In the public library, research newspaper articles which reported on the event. From these articles, piece together as complete a story as possible of this shipwreck and prepare an oral presentation for the class.

3. As a crew member on the *Edmund Fitzgerald*, you have kept a diary for many years. Only hours before the freighter sinks in the violent November gale, with little hope of rescue, you make your final entry in this diary. Write that entry.

4. The story of the *Bluenose* is one celebrated in Canadian history. Evidence for this is seen in the fact that the *Bluenose* has been commemorated on the Canadian dime. Research the facts about the famed Nova Scotian schooner and prepare a concise one-page report. Compare your report with that of a partner.

5. "The Ballad of the Bluenose" has been recorded. Listen to a recording of this ballad in class. Listen to other albums containing sea ballads from Atlantic Canada. Compare differences in renditions, if possible.

6. Write an imagined interview between you and William Henry Drummond that focusses on his life in Quebec, his love for French Canadians, and the humour in his poetry. To prepare to write, you will need to study more Drummond poetry and learn something of his life. When it is complete, dramatize your interview with a partner for your group or the class.

Robert William Service was born in England but spent his boyhood in Ayrshire, Scotland where he became fascinated by the romantic stories and poems of Sir Walter Scott and Robert Louis Stevenson. He was known as an imaginative, shy child who displayed a gift for rhyming at an early age. Service attended high school in Glasgow and apprenticed in the Commercial Bank of Scotland. During these years, he read widely and experimented with writing. Being captivated by rhyming, Service came to enjoy the work of poets such as Edgar Allan Poe.

Service came to Canada in 1886 in search of adventure and freedom. His early years in Canada were disappointing. He worked for two years as a farm labourer. He then tried his luck in San Francisco but, out of money, he lived most of his time there with bums and hobos. He travelled to Mexico and into the American South-West. For a period of several months in 1898, he took up singing and playing a guitar as he travelled through Colorado, Nevada, and Arizona. The loss of his guitar made him think of finding better paying work and, hence, he returned to British Columbia in 1899 to work on a large ranch.

Service found himself in the Yukon quite by accident. He had always wanted white-collar employment and so, in 1903, he took a position with the Canadian Bank of Commerce in Victoria, British Columbia. In 1904, he was transferred to Whitehorse. It was here that the bank teller Robert Service became the poet Robert Service of international renown.

In the Yukon, Service was surrounded by absorbing tales and all kinds of adventurous people. By applying to these tales and characters his love of romance and his skills as a rhymer and as an astute observer of human behaviour, Service produced the kind of poetry that he is still remembered for today. By 1909, he was a great literary triumph. His *Songs of a Sourdough* written at Whitehorse was the most successful book of poetry of its time. This collection contains such well-known ballads as "The Spell of the Yukon," "The Cremation of Sam McGee," and "The Shooting of Dan McGrew." Service travelled all through the North after this early success. He completed *Rhymes of a Rolling Stone* in Dawson. This book is a collection of ballads of the Mackenzie River basin and of the Arctic.

After he left the Yukon, Service worked briefly as a war correspondent for the *Toronto Star*. In 1916, Service enlisted as an ambulance driver for the Canadian Army Medical Corps. Another very successful collection of verse, *Rhymes of a Red Cross Man*, was written as a direct response to his experiences during the war years.

In 1921, Service went to Hollywood where his "The Shooting of Dan McGrew" was being made into a movie. During the twenties, he wrote several novels which were later scripted for Hollywood movies.

Service spent many of his subsequent years in France. In 1940, he escaped the Nazi occupation and again lived in the United States. After the war, Service returned to France where he spent most of his remaining years.

In addition to his poetry and novels, Service wrote two autobiographies, *Ploughman of the Moon* and *Harper of Heaven*. In all, he completed thirteen books of poetry and six novels. Service is best remembered for his dramatic ballads of the Yukon Gold Rush. His verses made him a household word in Canada, the United States, and Britain and earned him the wealth that afforded him the leisure to continue writing throughout his life. These ballads gave Service a public image as a rough burly old codger. In fact, he was a sensitive, romantic adventurer and a careful observer of human behaviour.

The Shooting of Dan McGrew

A bunch of the boys were whooping it up in the Malamute saloon;
The kid that handles the music-box was hitting a jag-time tune;
Back of the bar, in a solo game, sat Dangerous Dan McGrew,
And watching his luck was his light-o'-love, the lady that's known as Lou.

When out of the night, which was fifty below, and into the din
    and the glare,
There stumbled a miner fresh from the creeks, dog-dirty, and
    loaded for bear.
He looked like a man with a foot in the grave and scarcely the
    strength of a louse,
Yet he tilted a poke of dust on the bar, and called for drinks
    for the house.
There was none could place the stranger's face, though we
    searched ourselves for a clue;
But we drank his health, and the last to drink was Dangerous
    Dan McGrew.

There's men that somehow just grip your eyes, and hold them
    hard like a spell;
And such was he, and he looked to me like a man who had lived
    in hell;
With a face most hair, and the dreary stare of a dog whose day
    is done,
As he watered the green stuff in his glass, and the drops fell one
    by one.
Then I got to figgering who he was, and wondering what he'd
    do,
And I turned my head — and there watching him was the lady
    that's known as Lou.

His eyes went rubbering round the room, and he seemed in a
    kind of daze,
Till at last that old piano fell in the way of his wandering gaze.
The rag-time kid was having a drink; there was no one else on
    the stool,
So the stranger stumbles across the room, and flops down there
    like a fool.
In a buckskin shirt that was glazed with dirt he sat, and I saw
    him sway;
Then he clutched the keys with his talon hands — my God! but
    that man could play.

The Execution
Alden Nowlan

On the night of the execution
a man at the door
mistook me for the coroner.
'Press,' I said.

But he didn't understand. He led me
into the wrong room
where the sheriff greeted me:
'You're late, Padre.'

'You're wrong,' I told him. 'I'm Press.'
'Yes, of course, Reverend Press.'
We went down a stairway.

'Ah, Mr. Ellis,' said the Deputy.
'Press!' I shouted. But he shoved me
through a black curtain.
The lights were so bright
I couldn't see the faces
of the men sitting
opposite. But, thank God, I thought
they can see me!

'Look!' I cried. 'Look at my face!
Doesn't anybody know me?'

Then a hood covered my head.
'Don't make it harder for us,' the hangman whispered.

Focus on Meaning

1. a) Who is the speaker in "Porphyria's Lover"?
    What do we learn about him as he tells his
    tale?
    b) In pairs, write an interview between Por-
    phyria's lover and a police inspector investi-
    gating Porphyria's death. Then, with your
    partner, dramatize this interview for a small
    group or the class.

2. In what ways have the authors built and main-
    tained suspense in "The Raven" and in "Por-
    phyria's Lover"?

3. Memorize either "The Raven" or "Porphyria's
    Lover" and, in groups of four, recite your poem.
    You may want to recite it for the class as well.

4. In "At the Cedars," the storyteller must describe
    to a father the tragic death of his daughter. Have
    you ever had to tell a friend or a relative tragic
    news? Do you know anyone who has been in that
    situation? How does it feel to be the bearer of
    tragic news? How does one say the "right
    thing"? Tell the same sad story, as an eye-
    witness, in a letter to the father.

5. Setting in literature can be active, controlling to
    some extent the characters, or passive, simply
    enriching the action. How does setting con-
    tribute to the effect of "At the Cedars," "Por-
    phyria's Lover," and "The Raven"?

6. In groups of four, prepare one of the poems from
    the unit or another narrative poem on the same
    theme for reading aloud. Consider the effects of
    mood and rhythm as you plan your interpreta-
    tion. Use sound effects and tape your poem if
    you like. Share your interpretation with another
    group or with the entire class.

13 Tales to Chill Your Bones

Atwood has gained a reputation as one of Canada's most celebrated poets. One of her many volumes of poetry, *The Circle Game*, earned for her the Governor-General's Award in 1966. The subjects in her poems are frightened, isolated, alienated people. An insurmountable barrier always exists between her subjects and that for which they are striving. Her subjects tend to be pioneers, immigrants, or explorers who expend all their energies trying to survive in the hostile wilderness. They never seem to be able to master the power of nature and are left defeated and alone.

The style of Atwood's poetry is often prosaic and matter of fact. She shifts back and forth between rugged reality and fantasy and her line lengths seem haphazard.

A poem that is representative of Atwood's style is "Progressive Insanities of a Pioneer." In this poem, a pioneer struggles to establish himself, to bring order to a piece of wilderness and, despite his greatest efforts, is defeated by nature. There is a sense in this poem that no matter how hard the character strives, there is no key that will allow him to bring order to this confusion. Such are the themes that run through much of Atwood's work.

More recently, Atwood has written several novels, including *The Edible Woman, Surfacing,* and *Lady Oracle*. The themes and style of these works have much in common with those evident in her poetry.

Atwood presently lives in Toronto where she pursues her writing on a full-time basis.

Margaret Atwood was born of Nova Scotian parents in Ottawa in 1939. Her father was an entomologist who specialized in forest insects and hence Atwood spent much of her early life in the bush country of Northern Ontario and Quebec. She came to know the magnitude, the power, and the dominance of nature during these early years, influences that significantly affected her later writing.

Atwood graduated from the University of Toronto in 1961 and from Harvard in 1962. She taught English literature at the University of British Columbia in Vancouver, Sir George Williams University in Montreal, the University of Alberta in Edmonton, and York University in Toronto. She has also spent periods in her life in Boston and has travelled in England, France, and Italy. She served as Writer-in-Residence at the University of Toronto from 1972 to 1973.

From the Journals of Susanna Moodie:

Disembarking at Quebec

Is it my clothes, my way of walking,
the things I carry in my hand
— a book, a bag with knitting —
the incongruous pink of my shawl

this space cannot hear

or is it my own lack
of conviction which makes
these vistas of desolation,
long hills, the swamps, the barren sand, the glare
of sun on the bone-white
driftlogs, omens of winter,
the moon alien in day-
time a thin refusal

The others leap, shout

      Freedom!

The moving water will not show me
my reflection.

The rocks ignore.

I am a word
in a foreign language.

The Planters

They move between the jagged edge
of the forest and the jagged river
on a stumpy patch of cleared land

my husband, a neighbour, another man
weeding the few rows
of string beans and dusty potatoes.

They bend, straighten: the sun
lights up their faces and hands, candles
flickering in the wind against the

unbright earth. I see them: I know
none of them believe they are here.
They deny the ground they stand on,

pretend this dirt is the future.
And they are right. If they let go
of that illusion solid to them as a shovel,

open their eyes even for a moment
to these trees, to this particular sun
they would be surrounded, stormed, broken

in upon by branches, roots, tendrils, the dark
side of light
as I am.

Death of a Young Son by Drowning

He, who navigated with success
the dangerous river of his own birth
once more set forth

on a voyage of discovery
into the land I floated on
but could not touch to claim.

His feet slid on the bank,
the currents took him;
he swirled with ice and trees in the swollen water

and plunged into distant regions,
his head a bathysphere;
through his eyes' thin glass bubbles

he looked out, reckless adventurer
on a landscape stranger than Uranus
we have all been to and some remember.

Progressive Insanities of a Pioneer

I

He stood, a point
on a sheet of green paper
proclaiming himself the centre,

with no walls, no borders
anywhere; the sky no height
above him, totally un-
enclosed
and shouted:

Let me out!

II

He dug the soil in rows,
imposed himself with shovels
He asserted
into the furrows, I
am not random.

The ground
replied with aphorisms:

a tree-sprout, a nameless
weed, words
he couldn't understand.

III

The house pitched
the plot staked
in the middle of nowhere.

At night the mind
inside, in the middle
of nowhere.

The idea of an animal
patters across the roof.

In the darkness the fields
defend themselves with fences
in vain:
        everything
        is getting in.

IV

By daylight he resisted.
He said, disgusted
with the swamp's clamourings and the outbursts
of rocks,
        This is not order
        but the absence
        of order.

He was wrong, the unanswering
forest implied:
        It was
        an ordered absence.

V

For many years
he fished for a great vision,
dangling the hooks of sown
roots under the surface
of the shallow earth.

It was like
enticing whales with a bent
pin. Besides he thought

in that country
only the worms were biting.

VI

If he had known unstructured
space is a deluge
and stocked his log house-
boat with all the animals

even the wolves,

he might have floated.

But obstinate he
stated, The land is solid
and stamped,

watching his foot sink
down through stone
up to the knee.

VII

Things
refused to name themselves; refused
to let him name them.

The wolves hunted
outside.

On his beaches, his clearings,
by the surf of under-
growth breaking
at his feet, he foresaw
disintegration
          and in the end
through eyes
made ragged by his
effort, the tension
between subject and object,

the green vision,
the unnamed
whale invaded.

1. The poems in this chapter show a progression in the lives of two different pioneers. To what does each pioneer progress? How do they feel about where they end up at the end of these poems?

2. Have you ever experienced feelings similar to those expressed in these Atwood poems? Comment.

3. Organize a panel discussion about Atwood's poetry. The four or five students who join the panel should each read one of Atwood's poetry books and be prepared to discuss the work they selected in terms of subject, form, tone, diction, and imagery. A moderator could then be selected to facilitate the discussion.

4. To what extent does setting control the characters in these poems? Use specific examples from the poems to support your answer.

Shorter Lyric Poetry

A lyric poem is the most popular form of poetry — short and emotional. Such a poem is the most direct statement of a poet's deepest feeling; it grows out of his or her conviction that an experience — whether beautiful or painful — is worth expressing. The lyric was originally written to be sung and one of its prevailing characteristics is its melody. What was once achieved by the accompaniment of a musical instrument is now accomplished by a poet's skilful use of the sounds and rhythms of language.

Poets feel experience sharply. They are acutely aware of the world they live in: the beauty of a summer's day, the horrors of war, the love of one person for another, and the angers, sorrows, and pleasures of everyday living. Their art lies in their ability to translate these experiences into words, to experiment with the sounds and rhythms of language until they achieve their poems.

This unit will deal with short lyric poems, poems written according to a certain formula, and poems meant to be humorous or nonsensical.

Formula Poetry

A. The Haiku

William Wordsworth, the famous English poet, once defined poetry as "emotion recollected in tranquility." Japanese haiku fulfill that definition with significance and beauty. Anyone who has ever observed anything with a sense of wonder can write haiku.

Haiku is a form of verse invented in Japan centuries ago. The English interpretation of the Japanese haiku is three short lines of five, seven, and five syllables respectively. Translation of the Japanese haiku into English may result in more lines and syllables. The words speak of a mood, a strong feeling, or an atmosphere. Although the poem is usually about nature, a person's thoughts and emotions are often included.

The magic of good haiku lies in the power of suggestion. The general purpose of a haiku is to present one simple observation, and no more. But this one visual image creates a tension designed to make the reader think. This tension is usually produced by presenting a contrast and forcing the reader to make the connections between the seemingly disjointed parts of the image.

The impact of a haiku is like that of a pebble tossed into a stream. As you read the poem, it ripples your imagination, expanding and developing as you sense and share the experience of the poet.

Life Lesson
Don Raye

The fierce wind rages
And I see how trees survive —
They have learned to bend.

Inevitability
Don Raye

Homing geese, still winged,
Sliding down shafts of sunset
To join their shadows.

Understanding
Don Raye

A warm smile from you
Gleamed on me as a new moon —
It straightened things out.

New Year's Day
Basho

The first day of the year:
  thoughts come — and there is loneliness;
    the autumn dusk is here.

The Short Night
Buson

Night that ends so soon:
  in the ford there still remains
    one sliver of the moon.

Giddy Grasshopper
Issa

Giddy Grasshopper
Take care . . . Do not
Leap and crush
These pearls of dew-drop

Oh! I Ate Them All
Shiki

Oh! I ate them all
And oh! what a
Stomach-ache . . .
Green Stolen Apples

B. The Tanka

Tanka is another Japanese form of poem, and is almost like an extension of the haiku. The tanka adds two lines to the haiku, each of seven syllables. Thus it has five lines of thirty-one syllables used in the following way: 5, 7, 5, 7, and 7. Although the five lines of the Japanese tanka conform strictly to this breakdown in syllables, a tanka in English may consist of five lines without any specific number of syllables.

Tanka, like haiku, typically deal with a season of the year. Depth of meaning and striking imagery are of great importance in the tanka. Although these poems usually express serious ideas, it is possible to use humour if one wishes.

Adversity
Don Raye

Debris in the wind
Indiscriminately blinds
Eyes searching a path.
To turn one's back to the wind
Reveals but where one has been.

Papers
Anonymous

The pile of papers
Sprawled across this office desk
Are but memories
Of random skittery thoughts
Flitting past my vacant gaze.

C. The Cinquain

A cinquain is a short poem whose form was invented by Adelaide Crapsey, an American poet. A cinquain may be considered an English form of haiku or tanka, more suited to the rhythms of English. Crapsey developed the form for a five-line poem, in which the first line has two syllables, the second line has four, the third line has six, the fourth line has eight, and the fifth line ends the poem with two syllables. This form offers more than a simple syllabic arrangement. There is an elastic effect to it. The first four lines stretch; the final line snaps and releases. This startling factor throws the poem into harsh relief — the short last line with only two syllables makes noticeable impact.

A cinquain's lines can run on and it is often better if they do. A strong word ending each line gives the cinquain its balance and dignity. Its form is ideal for reflective thought.

In Adelaide Crapsey's skilled poet's hands, the cinquain became a subtle, sophisticated form.

Similarities
Anonymous

I touch
Two curving things:
The barrel of this pen,
The slow uncertain windings of
This verse.

The Warning
Adelaide Crapsey

Just now,
Out of the strange
Still dusk . . . as strange, as still . . .
A white moth flew. Why am I grown
So cold?

14 Formula Poetry

D. The Diamante

The diamante, a poetry pattern invented by Iris M. Tiedt, is a simple diamond-shaped poem expressing contrast. It may have any number of lines. The first line contains one word, the second two, the third three, and so on until the middle line, which introduces an idea opposite to the idea developed in the lines up to that point. Each line following the middle line decreases by one word until the last line, which consists of the direct opposite of the opening word.

In a seven-line diamante each of the following steps represents one line of the poem.
- one noun
- two adjectives describing the noun
- three participles (words that end in -ing or -ed) pertaining to the noun
- four nouns related to the subject (The second two nouns may have meanings opposite to the first two.)
- three participles indicating change or development of the subject noun
- two adjectives carrying on the idea of change or development
- a noun that is opposite to the original noun

The result is a seven-line contrast poem that has changed in meaning from beginning to end.

Joy —
Frisky, buoyant
Warming, sparkling, reveling
Nonsense, comedy — witchery, absurdity
Haunting, piercing, confusing
Doubtful, lonely
Grief.

Galaxies —
Distant, huge
Glowing, turning, going
Space, mystery — energy, life
Growing, circling, building
Tiny, basic
Atoms.

E. The Limerick

Another form of folk verse is the limerick. Like most forms of poetry, its specific origin remains baffling. The limerick supposedly began as a kind of song which was passed around orally. Although there were limericks in print as early as 1821, it was not until Edward Lear published his *Book of Nonsense* in 1846 that they achieved popularity. People today enjoy the limericks in Lear's *The Complete Nonsense Book* as well as the ones in William Jay Smith's *Typewriter Town* and Sara and John Brewton's *Laughable Limericks*. This favourite form of light verse, often nonsensical, frequently concerns people's actions, manners, and eccentricities.

The writer of limericks must be willing to follow a definite form of rhyme arrangement. To write verse with a definite rhythm to it, the writer must be sure that the accented or stressed beats in a poetic line fall on words or parts of words which are normally accented when they are pronounced. There must be just the right number of unaccented sounds between each accented sound so that the rhythm is right and natural, and forms a standard limerick line. The first, second, and fifth lines must have three accented beats to them. The third and fourth lines have two accented beats.

Besides the rhythmical pattern, a limerick must also have a definite rhyme scheme. The most common rhyme scheme is *aabba*.

Generally, in writing a limerick, a poet follows a specific pattern of thought. Each of the following steps represents one line of a limerick.
- Tell about the subject and where he or she is from.
- Tell something about the person or describe him or her.
- Build up (in lines 3 and 4) the peculiarity mentioned in the second line.
- Round off the limerick with an unexpected and funny conclusion, based on whatever has been talked about in the first four lines.

I remember a fellow named Louie
Who ate seventeen bowls of chop-suey;
When the eighteenth was brought,
He became overwrought
And we watched as poor Louie went blooie!

A lady from near Lake Louise
Declared she was bothered by fleas.
   She used gasoline
   And later was seen
Sailing over the hills and the trees.

I sat next the Duchess at tea.
It was just as I feared it would be:
   Her rumblings abdominal
   Were simply abominable,
And everyone thought it was me.

There was an old grouch from Ontario
Who purchased a thousand-watt stereo.
   When he turned it up loud
   He collected a crowd
And they strangled him with his own aerial.

Focus on Meaning

1. Some people feel that there are poems that are better left uninterpreted. Choose one of the types of poetry in this chapter and argue this point.

2. Which of the five types of poetry in this chapter are best for expressing the following: a feeling of being separate, a feeling of belonging, transforming from feelings of alienation to brotherhood, identity fears, humour, contrast, depth of emotion, love? Explain your answers.

A. The Epigram

An epigram is a brief, witty statement, usually in the form of a poem. This saying may be merely clever or it may be thought-provoking. This type of terse and witty poem ("Men seldom make passes/At girls who wear glasses." — Dorothy Parker) or statement ("Life is much too important a thing ever to talk seriously about." — Oscar Wilde) usually ends with an ingenious turn of thought.

In reading an epigram, one immediately notices that a lot of meaning and a great deal of experience and wisdom have been condensed into a compact, memorably balanced, emphatic expression. Epigrams aim at rapping out a tough thought by a flash of wit within a tightly closed form.

B. The Epitaph

An epitaph is an elegy for inscription on a monument. Because an epitaph originally was inscribed on a tombstone, it is brief. This short statement in memory of a dead person, usually put on his or her tombstone, is meant to sum up the life or outlook of the deceased. At its best, the epitaph is a moving expression of grief. In verse, however, many are light or even cynical. As can be seen in "For King Charles II," it is sometimes very difficult to distinguish between epigram and epitaph.

There are many examples of epitaphs in a number of poetry anthologies and many of them are amusing. They either comment on a person's life, character, profession, or manner of death, and often incorporate a play on words.

On His Books
Hilaire Belloc

When I am dead, I hope it may be said:
His sins were scarlet, but his books were read.

Sir, I Admit
Samuel Taylor Coleridge

Sir, I admit your general rule,
That every poet is a fool.
But you yourself may serve to show it,
That every fool is not a poet.

For King Charles II
John Wilmot, 2nd Earl of Rochester

Here lies our sovereign lord, the King,
Whose promise none relies on;
He never said a foolish thing,
Nor ever did a wise one.

Wit
Irving Layton

O you who read my epitaph,
Approve this final jest and laugh;
For if I stood where now stand you,
Believe me, friend, I would laugh too.

Crossing the Bar
Alfred, Lord Tennyson

Sunset and evening star,
    And one clear call for me!
And may there be no moaning of the bar,
    When I put out to sea,

But such a tide as moving seems asleep,
    Too full for sound and foam,
When that which drew from out the boundless deep
    Turns again home.

Twilight and evening bell,
    And after that the dark!
And may there be no sadness of farewell,
    When I embark;

For tho' from out our bourne of Time and Place
    The flood may bear me far,
I hope to see my Pilot face to face
    When I have crossed the bar.

On Frank Pixley, Editor
Ambrose Bierce

Here lies Frank Pixley, as usual.

Stop, Christian Passer-by!
Samuel Taylor Coleridge

STOP, Christian passer-by! — Stop, child of God,
And read with gentle breast. Beneath this sod
A poet lies, or that which once seem'd he.
O, lift one thought in prayer for S.T.C.;
That he who many a year with toil of breath
Found death in life, may here find life in death!
Mercy for praise — to be forgiven for fame
He ask'd, and hope, through Christ. Do thou the same!

Sacred to the Remains of
Anonymous

Sacred to the remains of
  Jonathan Thompson
  A pious Christian and
  Affectionate husband
    ● ● ●
His disconsolate widow
  Continues to carry on
  His grocery business
    At the old stand on
  Main Street; cheapest
And best prices in town

On the 22nd of June
Anonymous

On the 22nd of June
  Jonathan Fiddle
  Went out of tune

Focus on Meaning

1. Why do you think wit is better preserved in epigram form rather than in prose?

2. See if you can find the epitaphs of three famous or infamous people.

16 Nonsensical and Humorous Poetry

A great many poems are written just for fun. A poem which is both funny *and* a good poem is a tricky combination, for a good joke is funniest the first time it is heard, whereas a good poem gets better each time it is reread. Nevertheless, the humorous mode may well be the vehicle for poetry as serious, as intelligent, as beautiful, and as profound as poetry written in other, more "respectable" modes. In this chapter, you will find a few of the thousands of humorous poems that exist in English.

Often writers with a sense of humour like to play with words and ideas, even though the results do not seem to mean very much. This type of writing is called "nonsense," because it has little or no significance beyond the funny ideas presented.

---

cheerio my deario
(By archy the cockroach)
Don Marquis

well boss i met
mehitabel the cat
trying to dig a
frozen lamb chop
out of a snow
drift the other day

a heluva comedown
that is for me archy
she says a few
brief centuries
ago one of old
king
tut
ankh
amens favourite
queens and today
the village scavenger
but wotthehell
archy wotthehell
its cheerio
my deario that
pulls a lady through

see here mehitabel
i said i thought
you told me that
it was cleopatra
you used to be
before you
transmigrated into
the carcase of a cat
where do you get
this tut
ankh
amen stuff
question mark

i was several
ladies my little
insect says she
being cleopatra was
only an incident
in my career
and i was always getting
the rough end of it
always being
misunderstood by some
strait laced
prune faced bunch
of prissy mouthed
sisters of uncharity
the things that
have been said
about me archy
exclamation point

and all simply
because i was a
live dame
the palaces i have
been kicked out of
in my time
exclamation point

but wotthehell
little archy wot
thehell
its cheerio
my deario
that pulls a
lady through
exclamation point

framed archy always
framed that is the
story of all my lives
no chance for a dame
with the anvil chorus
if she shows a little
motion it seems to
me only yesterday
that the luxor local
number one of
the ladies axe
association got me in
dutch with king tut and
he slipped me the
sarcophagus always my
luck yesterday an empress
and today too
emaciated to interest
a vivisectionist but
toujours gai archy
toujours gai and always
a lady in spite of hell
and transmigration
once a queen
always a queen
archy
period

one of her
feet was frozen
but on the other three
she began to caper and
dance singing its
cheerio my deario
that pulls a lady
through her morals may
have been mislaid somewhere
in the centuries boss but
i admire her spirit
        archy

nobody loses all the time
e. e. cummings

nobody loses all the time

i had an uncle named
Sol who was a born failure and
nearly everybody said he should have gone
into vaudeville perhaps because my Uncle Sol could
sing McCann He Was A Diver on Xmas Eve like Hell itself which
may or may not account for the fact that my Uncle

Sol indulged in that possibly most inexcusable
of all to use a highfalootin phrase
luxuries that is or to
wit farming and be
it needlessly
added

my Uncle Sol's farm
failed because the chickens
ate the vegetables so
my Uncle Sol had a
chicken farm till the
skunks ate the chickens when

my Uncle Sol
had a skunk farm but
the skunks caught cold and
died and so
my Uncle Sol imitated the
skunks in a subtle manner

or by drowning himself in the watertank
but somebody who'd given my Uncle Sol a Victor
Victrola and records while he lived presented to
him upon the auspicious occasion of his decease a
scrumptious not to mention splendiferous funeral with
tall boys in black gloves and flowers and everything and

i remember we all cried like the Missouri
when my Uncle Sol's coffin lurched because
somebody pressed a button
(and down went
my Uncle
Sol

and started a worm farm)

Waiter! . . . There's an Alligator in My Coffee
Joe Rosenblatt

Waiter! . . . there's an alligator in my coffee.
Are you trying to be funny?
he said:
what do you want for a dime . . .?
. . . a circus?
but sir! I said,
he's swimming
around
and around
in my coffee
and he might
jump out on the table . . .
Feed him a lump of sugar! he snarled -
no! . . . make it two;
it'll weigh him down
and he'll drown.
I dropped two blocks of sugar
into the swamp
two grist jaws snapped them up
and the critter -
he never drowned.
Waiter! . . . there's an alligator in my coffee.
Kill him! Kill him!
he said:
BASH HIS BRAINS OUT
WITH YOUR SPOON . . .!
By this time
considerable attention had been drawn:
around my coffee
the waiters, the owner,
and customers gathered.
What seems to be the trouble?
the owner inquired,
and I replied:
There's an alligator in my coffee!
. . . But the coffee's fresh, he said
and raised the cup up to his nose . . .
Careful! I said.
he'll bite it
off
and he replied:
How absurd,
and lowered the cup
level to his mouth and
swallowed
the evidence.

Susan Simpson
Anonymous

Sudden swallows swiftly skimming,
    Sunset's slowly spreading shade,
Silvery songsters sweetly singing,
    Summer's soothing serenade.

Susan Simpson strolled sedately,
    Stifling sobs, suppressing sighs.
Seeing Stephen Slocum, stately
    She stopped, showing some surprise.

"Say," said Stephen, "sweetest sigher;
    Say, shall Stephen spouseless stay?"
Susan, seeming somewhat shyer,
    Showed submissiveness straightaway.

Summer's season slowly stretches,
    Susan Simpson Slocum she —
So she signed some simple sketches —
    Soul sought soul successfully.

****

Six Septembers Susan swelters;
    Six sharp seasons snow supplied;
Susan's satin sofa shelters
    Six small Slocums side by side.

Focus on Meaning

1. Using the poems in this chapter for ideas, choose some incidents for a humorous skit or for a cartoon illustration.

2. After you've finished reading e.e. cummings's unusual poem "nobody loses all the time," decide on what kind of a person the speaker's uncle Sol was. Write a short character sketch of this man who is not easily defeated.

3. What is humorous about the poem "Waiter! . . . There's an Alligator in my Coffee"?

is intended to do just one job: to make us see ourselves and the everyday world we live in — just as we are, just as it is — more clearly, more honestly than ever before.

Raymond Souster was born and raised in Toronto, the son of a bank clerk. He graduated from high school in 1939 and started work with the old Imperial Bank, which later merged with the Commerce. Apart from four years in the wartime RCAF (four crucial years in Souster's development as an adult and as a poet), he has worked there ever since. After the war he met and married a girl who was working in the bank. It was at this point that Souster turned his attention to writing. He soon became a leading figure in Canadian poetry.

Souster began writing poems before the war, but it wasn't until the fifties, back home in Toronto, that he developed the style he has since made his own. His concise, witty poems are often based on a single everyday incident. These poems, often in the form of short vignettes or lyrical portraits, champion the victims of impersonality and injustice. There is a peculiar importance of such figures as birds and flowers, beggars and cats (but never dogs), and above all, love and friendship. Souster's verses often present a simple experience; however, his gift for observation and his unique, briefly-stated style create a powerful image of truth.

Other than his own poetry, Raymond Souster — as editor and anthologist — has made many contributions to Canadian writing. He has been instrumental in the publishing of works by new Canadian poets. His two magazines, turned out on "a $35 hand-operated mimeograph machine," focussed important developments in contemporary poetry. These magazines, *Contact* and *Combustion*, have made 28 Mayfield Avenue an internationally-known address. As one of the editors (Louis Dudek and Irving Layton were the others) of Contact Press, Souster provided practically the only outlet for young Canadian poets during the fifties. As President of the League of Canadian Poets, Souster has worked to develop programs of poetry reading and writing throughout Canada.

Poets commonly either are or pretend to be different from other people. They see things more clearly, they feel things more intensely, they are "unique." Raymond Souster isn't at all like that. Though he's recognized by most critics as one of Canada's most significant poets, he's hard to distinguish from the man on the next stool at the neighbourhood restaurant. He wears suits, his hair is short, and he works every day at a Toronto Bank of Commerce at the corner of King and Bay. He has a wife and a home in Toronto's west end, where he grew up. He played organized baseball from his youth until he was forty-five — until his fastball started "hanging" and his curveball started "floating."

These are the facts it is wise to begin with, with Souster. They are central to all his poems. In these poems he shows us things that are already familiar. He is himself familiar — we can see him (or a reasonable facsimile) any day on any downtown street in Toronto or in Edmonton or Saskatoon or Winnipeg or Ottawa or Halifax. Every poem he writes

Flight of the Roller Coaster

Once more around should do it, the man confided . . .

and sure enough, when the roller-coaster reached the peak
of the giant curve above me, screech of its wheels
almost drowned out by the shriller cries of the riders,

instead of the dip and plunge with its landslide of screams,
it rose in the air like a movieland magic carpet,
    some wonderful bird,

and without fuss or fanfare swooped slowly across
    the amusement park,
over Spook's Castle, ice-cream booths, shooting-gallery.
    And losing no height

made the last yards above the beach, where the cucumber-cool
brakeman in the last seat saluted
a lady about to change from her bathing-suit.

Then, as many witnesses reported, headed leisurely
    out over the water,
disappearing all too soon behind a low-flying flight of clouds.

Orange Butterfly Lighting

Orange butterfly lighting
on the lowest branch
of my weeping-willow tree,
and hanging there motionless
for a moment's rest,

your time will be over
when those green leaves you clutch
turn to yellow and fall.

Yet you flutter away
with such bounce in your wings,
as if summer had arrived
only yesterday,

that you make me ashamed
of my life-to-death thoughts,
turn my face again to catch
the warm living heat
of the August sun.

The Top Hat

Whether it's just a gag or the old geezer's
a bit queer in the head, it's still refreshing
to see someone walking up Bay Street
with toes out of shoes, patched trousers, frayed suit-coat,
and on his head the biggest, shiniest top hat
since Abe Lincoln,
                and walking as if the whole
damn street belonged to him:
                        which at this moment for my money
it does.

Our Weeping-Willow

When we moved here, twelve years ago,
you were little more than a sapling,
a struggling one at that. I remember
how that first winter I despaired of your life,
especially that night of the ice-storm,
when you ended up face-down, icicle-frozen,
in the snow. If I hadn't lashed you upright
to a stake you would have died
right then, I'm sure of it.

Still, you somehow survived that winter, then another,
grew at first slowly in all the wrong directions,
a skinny, knock-kneed child. Then suddenly
you'd reached young manhood, threw out branches
more confidently, reaching out and up,
but always toward the sun. And just today I've noticed
you're even taller now than the house,
and I find it's all I can do
to stretch my arms around your trunk.

Well, there's no doubt of it,
you'll always be that much more
than just another tree to us,
for you're the sapling
I pulled up from death beneath the snow,
then coaxed back to life;
our love for you given back
in ten thousand leaves,
in a hundred swaying branches.

Minor Testament

Solzhenitsyn, as I learn
more and more about the miracle
of your life, its heights,
its utter desolations,

I grow more and more ashamed
of my own life, its pitiful
evasions, pretences, easy courage,

follow even further behind
the brilliance of your shadow.

Focus on Raymond Souster

1. Do you like the poem "Flight of the Roller Coaster"? What aspect of the poem do you like or dislike? Have you ever been in a situation where you let your imagination run away with you? Explain.

2. "The Top Hat" describes one of society's "misfits." Yet the speaker seems to look upon this individual in a much different light. Do you agree with the poet's perception of the man in the top hat? What do you think of people who are society's outcasts?

3. In "Orange Butterfly Lighting," the butterfly affects the speaker in quite a profound way. What do you think of his response to the butterfly? Have you ever been in a situation where some aspect of nature has made you sit back and think? Explain.

4. Why do you think the tree in "Our Weeping-Willow" is so important to the poet? Do you agree with this outlook on nature?

5. What conclusions can you draw from the poet's comparison of his life and that of Solzhenitsyn? Why do you think Souster wrote "Minor Testament"?

Longer Lyric Poetry

The two words, "lyric poetry," cover a wide range of poetry from shorter poems to longer ones, from light and humorous poems to deeper and more serious ones. Even as the length and content vary, so too do the forms. For lyric poetry includes the precise and specific forms of haiku or sonnet, as well as forms which have no specific definitions and which are as original as each individual poet.

A lyric poem presents personal emotion. Often this is joyful emotion, such as an expression of the joys of friendship, of love, or of reflection on the beautiful aspects of nature. However, not all of life's happenings are beautiful. Similarly, lyric poetry also deals with painful emotion — with the pain of friends parting and the resulting loneliness, with the pain of love gone amiss, with fears of the passage of time and the inescapable reality of death.

Some of the poems in this unit you will find quite easy to understand. For example, Pratt's meaning and emotion are straightforward in his poem "Erosion." It may take more imagination to feel as the poet feels in reading other poems, for example, to understand why the poet is so thrilled in "Jenny Kissed Me," or to pretend, with Shelley, that he is a cloud.

Many aspects of life are touched by the following poems, for lyric poetry confronts emotion and ideas which need to be confronted, which need to be expressed. The lyric poet touches all of us in such a way as to make us feel the depths and intensities of both real and imagined life's experience.

17 Love

Poets write of love in many ways. Sometimes they express sadness, sadness for love that is over, for lovers who are parted, for love that is not realized until it is too late. Sometimes the poet's mood is one of the most intense joy, arising from the fulfillment of deep and timeless love.

The poems in this chapter represent the great variety of lyrics written on the theme of love. Some of these lyric poems use images of startling beauty; others are ordinary, even plain. Some speak of enchantment; others are definitely realistic. And, although we usually associate the word "love" with romantic love, some of the poems go beyond mere conventional ideas we may have of love.

Whatever their words, whatever their moods, an expression of the emotion of a love experience is captured in the poets' lines.

Those Winter Sundays
Robert Hayden

Sundays too my father got up early
and put his clothes on in the blueblack cold,
then with cracked hands that ached
from labor in the weekday weather made
banked fires blaze. No one ever thanked him.

I'd wake and hear the cold splintering, breaking.
When the rooms were warm, he'd call,
and slowly I would rise and dress,
fearing the chronic angers of that house,

Speaking indifferently to him,
who had driven out the cold
and polished my good shoes as well.
What did I know, what did I know
of love's austere and lonely offices?

She Walks in Beauty
George Gordon, Lord Byron

She walks in beauty, like the night
    Of cloudless climes and starry skies;
And all that's best of dark and bright
    Meet in her aspect and her eyes:
Thus mellow'd to that tender light
    Which Heaven to gaudy day denies.

One shade the more, one ray the less,
    Had half impair'd the nameless grace
Which waves in every raven tress,
    Or softly lightens o'er her face;
Where thoughts serenely sweet express
    How pure, how dear their dwelling-place.

And on that cheek, and o'er that brow,
    So soft, so calm, yet eloquent,
The smiles that win, the tints that glow,
    But tell of days in goodness spent,
A mind at peace with all below,
    A heart whose love is innocent!

The Taxi
Amy Lowell

When I go away from you
The world beats dead
Like a slackened drum.
I call out for you against the jutted stars
And shout into the ridges of the wind.
Streets coming fast,
One after the other,
Wedge you away from me,
And the lamps of the city prick my eyes
So that I can no longer see your face.
Why should I leave you,
To wound myself upon the sharp edges of the night?

Annabel Lee
Edgar Allan Poe

It was many and many a year ago,
    In a kingdom by the sea,
That a maiden there lived whom you may know
    By the name of ANNABEL LEE;
And this maiden she lived with no other thought
    Than to love and be loved by me.

I was a child and *she* was a child,
    In this kingdom by the sea,
But we loved with a love that was more than love —
    I and my ANNABEL LEE —
With a love that wingèd seraphs of heaven
    Coveted her and me.

And this was the reason that, long ago,
    In this kingdom by the sea,
A wind blew out of a cloud, chilling
    My beautiful ANNABEL LEE,
So that her high-born kinsmen came
    And bore her away from me,
To shut her up in a sepulchre
    In this kingdom by the sea.

The angels, not half so happy in heaven,
    Went envying her and me —
Yes! — that was the reason (as all men know,
    In this kingdom by the sea)
That the wind came out of the cloud by night,
    Chilling and killing my ANNABEL LEE.

But our love it was stronger by far than the love
    Of those who were older than we —
    Of many far wiser than we —
And neither the angels in heaven above,
    Nor the demons down under the sea,
Can ever dissever my soul from the soul
    Of the beautiful ANNABEL LEE:

For the moon never beams, without bringing me dreams
    Of the beautiful ANNABEL LEE:
And the stars never rise, but I feel the bright eyes
    Of the beautiful ANNABEL LEE:
And so, all the night-tide, I lie down by the side
Of my darling — my darling — my life and my bride,
    In the sepulchre there by the sea —
    In her tomb by the sounding sea.

For Anne
Leonard Cohen

With Annie gone,
whose eyes compare
With the morning sun?

Not that I did compare,
But I do compare
Now that she's gone.

Psyche with the Candle
Archibald MacLeish

Love which is the most difficult mystery
Asking from every young one answers
And most from those most eager and most beautiful —
Love is a bird in a fist:
To hold it hides it, to look at it lets it go.
It will twist loose if you lift so much as a finger.
It will stay if you cover it — stay but unknown and
    invisible.
Either you keep it forever with fist closed
Or let it fling
Singing in fervor of sun and in song vanish.
There is no answer other to this mystery.

Love Is Not All
Edna St. Vincent Millay

Love is not all: it is not meat nor drink
Nor slumber nor a roof against the rain;
Nor yet a floating spar to men that sink
And rise and sink and rise and sink again;
Love can not fill the thickened lung with breath,
Nor clean the blood, nor set the fractured bone;
Yet many a man is making friends with death
Even as I speak, for lack of love alone.
It well may be that in a difficult hour,
Pinned down by pain and moaning for release,
Or nagged by want past resolution's power,
I might be driven to sell your love for peace,
Or trade the memory of this night for food.
It well may be. I do not think I would.

Shall I Compare Thee to a Summer's Day?
William Shakespeare

Shall I compare thee to a summer's day?
Thou art more lovely and more temperate.
Rough winds do shake the darling buds of May,
And summer's lease hath all too short a date:
Sometime too hot the eye of heaven shines,
And often is his gold complexion dimm'd;
And every fair from fair some time declines,
By chance, or nature's changing course, untrimm'd;
But thy eternal summer shall not fade
Nor lose possession of that fair thou ow'st;
Nor shall Death brag thou wand'rest in his shade,
When in eternal lines to time thou grow'st.
   So long as men can breathe or eyes can see,
   So long lives this, and this gives life to thee.

Focus on Meaning

1. a) What does each of the following words — daylight, sunlight, starlight, moonlight, night — suggest to you in terms of beauty or lack of beauty? What feelings does each suggest to you?
    b) Re-read the poems in this section. How have the poets used these various images? What could you say to any of these poets in a discussion of their ideas? What suggestions could you make for possible changes in their images?

2. How does "Those Winter Sundays" differ from the other poems in this section? Express, in your own words, what this poem says about love.

3. Edgar Allan Poe defined poetry as "the rhythmical creation of beauty." After reading and studying his poem "Annabel Lee," what do you think he meant by this?

4. "Psyche with the Candle" can be understood without knowing the story from Greek mythology of Psyche. But that story is a fascinating one about a beautiful young girl, two jealous older sisters, the even more jealous goddess Venus and, in the midst of all this, a tender love. To know the story of Psyche is to understand more fully what MacLeish is saying.
    a) Find and read the story of Psyche. Make notes on the characters involved, and on the basic outline of the plot of the story.
    b) Using your notes, work in groups to prepare storyboards for a contemporary version of the story for a television movie.

5. a) In the sonnet "Love is Not All," Millay suggests that there are a lot of important things that love is not, or that love cannot do. What are some of these? Overall, what are Millay's ideas about the importance of love?
    b) Create your own statement of your own ideas of the importance of love. Gather pictures and words and titles from old magazines, and assemble, in pictorial rather than sonnet form, your own expression of the importance of love. Show, as you see them, two sides of love — the important things love cannot do, and the important things love can do.

6. William Shakespeare wrote 154 sonnets. Do research to find other sonnets he wrote. Read a few of them until you find one that you like. Bring it to class, and be ready to present it orally, and to discuss what you feel Shakespeare is saying in his sonnet.

Time, Change, and Memory

Time has concerned people since earliest history. They wonder, how can time be measured? How can time be stopped? Why can't time be hurried or slowed? What will happen in my future? These are often the poet's concerns as well.

Sometimes a poem looks back, recalling the past with countless different associations and emotions. Or, a poem may focus on through the past and present to the future. For the poet, perhaps more than any of us, realizes and can express the idea that in the larger scope of things, all time is one.

The poet writes of time as it is related to change, to growing, to growing up, to growing old. With time and change come the things that memories are made of, and the poet writes of these as well.

Memory
David Helwig

In the first evenings
when we walked together
spring had taken the city
by the hand.

We would walk silent or speaking
down a dozen unknown streets
of clustered houses
while the night was soft as lips
upon our skin.

As we walked through the dark,
lighted windows
made mysteries, made
a hundred private worlds.

Now in a house
where children sleep
we live within the light
and from our window
see sometimes
the shapes of lovers in the evening streets.

Song for Naomi
Irving Layton

Who is that in the tall grasses singing
By herself, near the water?
I can not see her
But can it be her
Than whom the grasses so tall
Are taller,
My daughter,
My lovely daughter?

Who is that in the tall grasses running
Beside her, near the water?
She can not see there
Time that pursued her
In the deep grasses so fast
And faster
And caught her,
My foolish daughter.

What is the wind in the fair grass saying
Like a verse, near the water?
Saviours that over
All things have power
Make Time himself grow kind
And kinder
That sought her,
My little daughter.

Who is that at the close of the summer
Near the deep lake? Who wrought her
Comely and slender?
Time but attends and befriends her
Than whom the grasses though tall
Are not taller,
My daughter,
My gentle daughter.

Journey of the Magi
T. S. Eliot

"A cold coming we had of it,
Just the worst time of the year
For a journey, and such a long journey:
The ways deep and the weather sharp,
The very dead of winter."
And the camels galled, sore-footed, refractory,
Lying down in the melting snow.
There were times we regretted
The summer palaces on slopes, the terraces,
And the silken girls bringing sherbet.
Then the camel men cursing and grumbling
And running away, and wanting their liquor and women,
And the night-fires going out, and the lack of shelters,
And the cities hostile and the towns unfriendly
And the villages dirty and charging high prices:
A hard time we had of it.
At the end we preferred to travel all night,
Sleeping in snatches,
With the voices singing in our ears, saying
That this was all folly.

Then at dawn we came down to a temperate valley,
Wet, below the snow line, smelling of vegetation;
With a running stream and a water-mill beating the darkness,
And three trees on the low sky,
And an old white horse galloped away in the meadow.
Then we came to a tavern with vine-leaves over the lintel,
Six hands at an open door dicing for pieces of silver,
And feet kicking the empty wine-skins.
But there was no information, and so we continued
And arrived at evening, not a moment too soon
Finding the place; it was (you may say) satisfactory.

All this was a long time ago, I remember,
And I would do it again, but set down
This set down
This: were we led all that way for
Birth or Death? There was a Birth, certainly,
We had evidence and no doubt. I had seen birth and death,
But had thought they were different; this Birth was
Hard and bitter agony for us, like Death, our death.
We returned to our places, these Kingdoms,
But no longer at ease here, in the old dispensation,
With an alien people clutching their gods.
I should be glad of another death.

To a Poet a Thousand Years Hence
James Elroy Flecker

I who am dead a thousand years,
    And wrote this sweet archaic song,
Send you my words for messengers
    The way I shall not pass along.

I care not if you bridge the seas,
    Or ride secure the cruel sky,
Or build consummate palaces
    Of metal or of masonry.

But have you wine and music still,
    And statues and a bright-eyed love,
And foolish thoughts of good and ill,
    And prayers to them who sit above?

How shall we conquer? Like a wind
    That falls at eve our fancies blow,
And old Maeonides the blind
    Said it three thousand years ago.

O friend unseen, unborn, unknown,
    Student of our sweet English tongue,
Read out my words at night, alone:
    I was a poet, I was young.

Since I can never see your face,
    And never shake you by the hand,
I send my soul through time and space
    To greet you. You will understand.

When You Are Old
William Butler Yeats

When you are old and gray and full of sleep,
And nodding by the fire, take down this book,
And slowly read, and dream of the soft look
Your eyes had once, and of their shadows deep;

How many loved your moments of glad grace,
And loved your beauty with love false or true;
But one man loved the pilgrim soul in you,
And loved the sorrows of your changing face.

And bending down beside the glowing bars,
Murmur, a little sadly, how love fled
And paced upon the mountains overhead
And hid his face amid a crowd of stars.

Jenny Kissed Me
Leigh Hunt

Jenny kissed me when we met,
Jumping from the chair she sat in;
Time, you thief, who love to get
Sweets into your list, put that in!
Say I'm weary, say I'm sad,
Say that health and wealth have missed me,
Say I'm growing old, but add,
Jenny kissed me.

Remember
Christina Rossetti

Remember me when I am gone away,
Gone far away into the silent land;
When you can no more hold me by the hand,
Nor I half turn to go, yet turning stay.
Remember me when no more, day by day,
You tell me of our future that you planned:
Only remember me; you understand
It will be late to counsel then or pray.
Yet if you should forget me for a while
And afterwards remember, do not grieve:
For if the darkness and corruption leave
A vestige of the thoughts that once I had,
Better by far you should forget and smile
Than that you should remember and be sad.

The Circle Game
Joni Mitchell

Yesterday a child came out to wander,
Caught a dragonfly inside a jar,
Fearful when the sky was full of thunder
And tearful at the falling of a star.

Chorus:
And the seasons they go 'round and 'round,
Painted ponies they go up and down,
We're captive in a carousel of time,
We can't return, we can only look
Behind from where we came
And go 'round and 'round and 'round in the circle game.

Then the child moved ten times 'round the seasons,
Skated over ten clear frozen streams.
Words like "When you're older" must appease him
And promises of "Someday" make his dreams.

Sixteen springs and sixteen summers gone now,
Cartwheels lost to carwheels through the town,
And you tell him "Take your time, it won't be long now
'Til you drag your feet to slow the circle down."

So the boy who dreamed tomorrow now is twenty,
And his dreams have lost some grandeur coming true;
There'll be new dreams maybe better dreams and plenty
Before the last revolving year is through.

Elegy: The Wood Is Bare

Robert Bridges

The wood is bare: a river-mist is steeping
    The trees that winter's chill of life bereaves:
Only their stiffened boughs break silence, weeping
      Over their fallen leaves;

That lie upon the dank earth brown and rotten,
    Miry and matted in the soaking wet:
Forgotten with the spring, that is forgotten
      By them that can forget.

Yet it was here we walked when ferns were springing,
    And through the mossy bank shot bud and blade: —
Here found in summer, when the birds were singing,
      A green and pleasant shade.

'Twas here we loved in sunnier days and greener;
    And now, in this disconsolate decay,
I come to see her where I most have seen her,
      And touch the happier day.

For on this path, at every turn and corner,
    The fancy of her figure on me falls;
Yet walks she with the slow step of a mourner,
      Nor hears my voice that calls.

So through my heart there winds a track of feeling,
    A path of memory, that is all her own:
Whereto her phantom beauty ever stealing
      Haunts the sad spot alone.

About her steps the trunks are bare, the branches
    Drip heavy tears upon her downcast head;
And bleed from unseen wounds that no sun stanches,
      For the year's sun is dead.

And dead leaves wrap the fruits that summer planted:
    And birds that love the South have taken wing.
The wanderer, loitering o'er the scene enchanted,
      Weeps, and despairs of spring.

Elegy for the South Valley

Pat Lowther

1
South Valley Dam is silted up,
the slid scree of a whole mountain
is leaning there; some year
when the rains keep
on and on as they do
it will go, and the wind seethe
in the trees,
the cedars toss and toss
and the creek froth
over broken banks
and the work of men
will be all undone

2
We have no centuries
here a few generations
do for antiquity:
logging camps hidden
around the backs of mountains
shacks falling without sound
canyons with timber trestles
rotting to shreds
like broken spiderwebs
straight scars and planks
collapsed on the walls
of improbable mountains
mountains mountains
and the dam that served
a mine that serviced empire
crumbling slowly deep
deep in the bush
for its time
for this country
it's a pyramid
it's Tenochtitlan going back
to the bush and the rain

3

The gravel pit is eating
South Valley, the way you'd
eat a stalk of asparagus,
end to end, saving the tender
tip for last. It starts
at the highway end
gouging alder and huckleberry
off the creek banks;
dust loosed in the air
precipitates slowly on water
and smooth wet stones.
Each year the tooth marks
go deeper along the valley
higher into the green
overhanging falls and terraces
of water, shearing toward
the head of the south fork
where the dam leans
between time's jaws
waiting for either
the weight of its past
or the hard bite of the future
to bring it down unmade
and original gravel
bury its shards at last.

Focus on Meaning

1. Read "Memory" carefully. What establishes the mood of Helwig's poem? What is your emotional response to it? Does your response differ from others in your class? How?

2. a) How has time affected Naomi in Layton's poem? How does the poet express these changes? Explain, in your own words, what he is saying about time.
   b) Pretend you are Naomi. In a creative composition, reflect on or show the changes of time as they affect your father.

3. a) What is the central event of Eliot's poem? What are the clues which tell you this?
   b) The speaker of this poem has undergone a great change in his lifetime. What is that change? Find lines which show how it has affected him and how it has affected those around him.

4. a) What kinds of change does Flecker not care about in "To A Poet a Thousand Years Hence"? What does he care about knowing? What message does he have for his reader? How does it differ from that in "The Circle Game"?
   b) Make a list of specific changes there have been in the world in the past thousand years. If you were to leave a message for someone to find "a thousand years hence," which of these changes would you want to tell about? Explain your answer.

5. In the poem "When You Are Old," Yeats reveals a little about the person to whom he addresses the poem. In a paragraph, characterize her — trying to determine what she is like when young, and what she is like when old.

6. What is your impression of the poem "Jenny Kissed Me"? What impression does it give you of the poet?

7. The poem "Remember" begins with a very strong opening statement. "Remember me when I am gone away." How does the poet want to be remembered? Do you agree with her, or would you want to be remembered in another way? Why?

8. What is Robert Bridges remembering in his elegy? How does he use imagery from nature in his poem? Do you think the setting of his poem is effective? Why?

9. Express the theme of "Elegy for the South Valley" in a sentence or two.

Death is a frequent theme in lyric poetry. Why? Because a poet is never afraid to write about those feared or mighty themes that touch us all. A poet has the uncanny ability to take our inexpressible thoughts and express them in a way that ordinary language cannot.

The deaths that poets write of may be personal and private, or they may be more general, even universal. For example, a poet may explore the emotion evoked by the death of a special person, or else explore the implications of the deaths of many, as in a wartime setting. Frequently, the dead person may be the speaker of the poem, and this can lead the poetic imagination to some startling effects.

Trying to understand the awesomeness of death is part of every person's life. The poet, in writing of death, speaks to us of life.

The Coffins
James Reaney

These coffins are submarines
That will sail beneath the slopes
Of gray-green old graveyards.

One white lone sailor to each
Submarine that navigates
The wormy seas of earth.

With shrouds for uniforms
Stitched by weeping tailors
These bony sailors
Shall sail deep field and morass
Without periscope or compass
They'll only dimly know
That someday they must flow
Into the final harbor
On some high gray shore
Where the Lord shall weigh
Men's wicked souls on Doomsday.

Do Not Go Gentle into That Good Night
Dylan Thomas

Do not go gentle into that good night,
Old age should burn and rave at close of day;
Rage, rage against the dying of the light.

Though wise men at their end know dark is right,
Because their words had forked no lightning they
Do not go gentle into that good night.

Good men, the last wave by, crying how bright
Their frail deeds might have danced in a green bay,
Rage, rage against the dying of the light.

Wild men who caught and sang the sun in flight,
And learn, too late, they grieved it on its way,
Do not go gentle into that good night.

Grave men, near death, who see with blinding sight
Blind eyes could blaze like meteors and be gay,
Rage, rage against the dying of the light.

And you, my father, there on the sad height,
Curse, bless, me now with your fierce tears, I pray.
Do not go gentle into that good night.
Rage, rage against the dying of the light.

Erosion
E. J. Pratt

It took the sea a thousand years,
A thousand years to trace
The granite features of this cliff,
In crag and scarp and base.

It took the sea an hour one night,
An hour of storm to place
The sculpture of these granite seams
Upon a woman's face.

The Soldier
Rupert Brooke

If I should die, think only this of me:
    That there's some corner of a foreign field
That is forever England. There shall be
    In that rich earth a richer dust concealed;
A dust whom England bore, shaped, made aware,
    Gave, once, her flowers to love, her ways to roam,
A body of England's, breathing English air,
    Washed by the rivers, blest by suns of home.

And think, this heart, all evil shed away,
    A pulse in the eternal mind, no less
        Gives somewhere back the thoughts by England given;
Her sights and sound; dreams happy as her day;
    And laughter, learnt of friends; and gentleness,
        In hearts at peace, under an English heaven.

In Flanders Fields
John McCrae

In Flanders fields the poppies blow
Between the crosses, row on row,
    That mark our place; and in the sky
    The larks, still bravely singing, fly
Scarce heard amid the guns below.

We are the Dead. Short days ago
We lived, felt dawn, saw sunset glow,
    Loved and were loved, and now we lie,
    In Flanders fields.

Take up our quarrel with the foe:
To you from failing hands we throw
    The torch, be yours to hold it high.
    If ye break faith with us who die
We shall not sleep, though poppies grow
    In Flanders fields.

A Satirical Elegy on the
Death of a Late Famous General
Jonathan Swift

    His Grace! impossible! what, dead!
Of old age too, and in his bed!

And could that Mighty Warrior fall?
And so inglorious, after all!
Well, since he's gone, no matter how,
The last loud trump must wake him now:

And, trust me, as the noise grows stronger,
He'd wish to sleep a little longer.
And could he be indeed so old
As by the newspapers we're told?
Threescore, I think, is pretty high;
'Twas time in conscience he should die.
This world he cumbered long enough;
He burnt his candle to the snuff;
And that's the reason, some folks think,
He left behind so great a stink.

Behold his funeral appears,
Nor widow's sighs, nor orphan's tears,
Wont at such times each heart to pierce,
Attend the progress of his hearse.
But what of that, his friends may say,
He had those honors in his day.
True to his profit and his pride,
He made them weep before he died.

    Come hither, all ye empty things,
Ye bubbles raised by breath of Kings;
Who float upon the tide of state,
Come hither, and behold your fate.
Let pride be taught by this rebuke,
How very mean a thing's a Duke;
From all his ill-got honors flung,
Turned to that dirt from whence he sprung.

19 Death

The Fox
Kenneth Patchen

Because the snow is deep
Without spot that white falling through white air

Because she limps a little — bleeds
Where they shot her

Because hunters have guns
And dogs have hangmen's legs

Because I'd like to take her in my arms
And tend her wound

Because she can't afford to die
Killing the young in her belly

I don't know what to say of a soldier's dying
Because there are no proportions in death.

Elegy Written in the Tower
Chidiock Tichborne

My prime of youth is but a frost of cares,
  My feast of joy is but a dish of pain,
My crop of corn is but a field of tares,
  And all my good is but vain hope of gain;
    The day is past, and yet I saw no sun,
    And now I live, and now my life is done.

My tale was heard and yet it was not told,
  My fruit is fallen and yet my leaves are green,
My youth is spent and yet I am not old,
  I saw the world and yet I was not seen;
    My thread is cut and yet it is not spun,
    And now I live, and now my life is done.

I sought my death and found it in my womb,
  I looked for life and saw it was a shade,
I trod the earth and knew it was my tomb,
  And now I die, and now I was but made;
    My glass is full, and now my glass is run,
    And now I live, and now my life is done.

Focus on Meaning

1. Think about yourself, your attitudes, your goals, and your priorities in life. Into which category of Thomas' poem — wise, good, wild, grave — do you best fit? What additional categories could he have used?

2. Both "In Flanders Fields" and "The Soldier" were written by wartime poets. What ideas or techniques do these poems share? How do they differ from each other? Which do you think is the better poem? Why?

3. a) What would a conventional elegy about the death of a famous warrior or general stress?

   b) What ideas or statements do you think are the most effective in Swift's satirical elegy? Why?

4. What does Kenneth Patchen say of death in his poem "The Fox"? In your own words, write a statement he might make to either John McCrae or Rupert Brooke.

5. a) Chidiock Tichborne was put to death in 1586 for conspiring against Queen Elizabeth I. Do some research on this exciting but often very bloody time in history to look up the stories of Queen Elizabeth I and her cousin Mary Queen of Scots. Try to find stories of others who were put to death for similar conspiracies.

   b) Tichborne's elegy was written approximately four hundred years ago. Is there anything in the poem which you think dates it? If so, what? What ideas seem modern and fresh? Why?

6. Even though a poem is about death, it should still make one think about life. Discuss this statement, on the basis of your reactions to the poems in this chapter.

20 Nature

The poems in this chapter are varied, but all are drawn from moods in nature. Nature, of course, suggests different things to different people. It may mean expanses of mountains, of forests seemingly untouched by human hands — but it may also mean a small walled garden in the centre of a city, a park at the edge of the road, or even a blade of grass struggling for life in a parking lot.

Nature provides the poet with descriptive images, but the poet may choose to move beyond description to deeper reflection. Inspiration from nature may come from the extraordinary, but more frequently it comes from familiar or reliable occurrences in nature. These provide insights about life, but also speak of constancy or stability in an ever-changing world.

One would have to search for a long time to find someone who does not feel even the slightest lift in spirits in response to beauty in nature. A sunrise, a sunset, the changes of the seasons, the majesty of a granite mountain, the calm of a still lake — all these and more speak to us of something greater than ourselves. Small wonder, then, that much of the mightiest lyric poetry is inspired by nature.

A Vagabond Song
Bliss Carman

There is something in the autumn that is native to my
    blood —
Touch of manner, hint of mood;
And my heart is like a rhyme,
With the yellow and the purple and the crimson keeping
    time.

The scarlet of the maples can shake me like a cry
Of bugles going by.
And my lonely spirit thrills
To see the frosty asters like a smoke upon the hills.

There is something in October sets the gypsy blood astir;
We must rise and follow her,
When from every hill of flame
She calls and calls each vagabond by name.

The Blue Heron
Theodore Goodridge Roberts

In a green place lanced through
With amber and gold and blue;
A place of water and weeds
And roses pinker than dawn,
And ranks of lush young reeds,
And grasses straightly withdrawn
From graven ripples of sands,
The still blue heron stands.

Smoke-blue he is, and grey
As embers of yesterday.
Still he is, as death;
Like stone, or shadow of stone,
Without a pulse or breath,
Motionless and alone
There in the lily stems:
But his eyes are alive like gems.

Still as a shadow; still
Grey feather and yellow bill:
Still as an image made
Of mist and smoke half hid
By windless sunshine and shade,
Save when a yellow lid
Slides and is gone like a breath:
Death-still — and sudden as death!

Solitude
Archibald Lampman

How still it is here in the woods. The trees
Stand motionless, as if they did not dare
To stir, lest it should break the spell. The air
Hangs quiet as spaces in a marble frieze.
Even this little brook, that runs at ease,
Whispering and gurgling in its knotted bed,
Seems but to deepen, with its curling thread
Of sound, the shadowy sun-pierced silences.
Sometimes a hawk screams or a woodpecker
Startles the stillness from its fixèd mood
With his loud careless tap. Sometimes I hear
The dreamy white-throat from some far off tree
Pipe slowly on the listening solitude,
His five pure notes succeeding pensively.

A November Landscape
E. J. Pratt

November came today and seized the whole
Of the autumnal store of reds, and left
But drabs and yellows on a land bereft
Of bird and leaf, of body and of soul.

Outside my window now rain-winds patrol
The earth; last August elms and birches seem
Like half-remembered legends in a dream;
Melodious myths — the Thrush and Oriole —

Such strange delusions when November weaves
The sense of desolation and regret
Through clay and stubble, through dead ferns and
     leaves
As here lie sodden on the ground; and yet

This was the story told six months ago,
When April lured the crocus through the snow.

Velvet Shoes
Elinor Wylie

Let us walk in the white snow
    In a soundless space;
With footsteps quiet and slow,
    At a tranquil pace,
Under veils of white lace.

I shall go shod in silk,
    And you in wool,
White as white cow's milk,
    More beautiful
    Than breast of gull.

We shall walk through the still town
    In a windless peace;
We shall step upon white down,
    Upon silver fleece,
    Upon softer than these.

We shall walk in velvet shoes:
    Wherever we go
Silence will fall like dews
    On white silence below.
    We shall walk in the snow.

I Wandered Lonely as a Cloud
William Wordsworth

I wandered lonely as a cloud
That floats on high o'er vales and hills,
When all at once I saw a crowd,
A host, of golden daffodils,
Beside the lake, beneath the trees,
Fluttering and dancing in the breeze.

Continuous as the stars that shine
And twinkle on the milky way,
They stretch'd in never-ending line
Along the margin of a bay:
Ten thousand saw I at a glance
Tossing their heads in sprightly dance.

The waves beside them danced, but they
Out-did the sparkling waves in glee: —
A Poet could not but be gay
In such a jocund company!
I gazed — and gazed — but little thought
What wealth the show to me had brought:

For oft, when on my couch I lie
In vacant or in pensive mood,
They flash upon that inward eye
Which is the bliss of solitude;
And then my heart with pleasure fills
And dances with the daffodils.

Snow
Louis MacNeice

The room was suddenly rich and the great
    bay-window was
Spawning snow and pink roses against it
Soundlessly collateral and incompatible:
World is suddener than we fancy it.

World is crazier and more of it than we think,
Incorrigibly plural. I peel and portion
A tangerine and spit the pips and feel
The drunkenness of things being various.

And the fire flames with a bubbling sound for world
Is more spiteful and gay than one supposes —
On the tongue on the eyes on the ears in the palms
    of one's hands —
There is more than glass between the snow and the
    huge roses.

A Bird Came Down the Walk
Emily Dickinson

A bird came down the walk:
He did not know I saw;
He bit an angle-worm in halves
And ate the fellow, raw.

And then he drank a dew
From a convenient grass,
And then hopped sidewise to the wall
To let a beetle pass.

He glanced with rapid eyes
That hurried all abroad, —
They looked like frightened beads, I thought
He stirred his velvet head

Like one in danger; cautious,
I offered him a crumb,
And he unrolled his feathers
And rowed him softer home

Than oars divide the ocean,
Too silver for a seam,
Or butterflies, off banks of noon,
Leap, plashless, as they swim.

The Cloud
Percy Bysshe Shelley

I bring fresh showers for the thirsting
    flowers,
    From the seas and the streams;
I bear light shade for the leaves when
    laid
    In their noonday dreams.
From my wings are shaken the dews
    that waken
    The sweet buds every one,
When rocked to rest on their mother's
    breast,
    As she dances about the sun.
I wield the flail of the lashing hail,
    And whiten the green plains under,
And then again I dissolve it in rain,
    And laugh as I pass in thunder.

I sift the snow on the mountains below,
    And their great pines groan aghast;
And all the night 'tis my pillow white,
    While I sleep in the arms of the blast.
Sublime on the towers of my skyey
    bowers
    Lightning my pilot sits;
In a cavern under is fettered the thun-
    der,
    It struggles and howls at fits;
Over earth and ocean, with gentle mo-
    tion,
This pilot is guiding me,
Lured by the love of the genii that move
    In the depths of the purple sea;
Over the rills, and the crags, and the
    hills,
    Over the lakes and the plains,
Wherever he dream, under mountain or
    stream,
    The Spirit he loves remains;
And I all the while bask in Heaven's
    blue smile,
    Whilst he is dissolving in rains.
The sanguine Sunrise, with his meteor
    eyes,
    And his burning plumes outspread,
Leaps on the back of my sailing rack,
    When the morning star shines dead;
As on the jag of a mountain crag,
    Which an earthquake rocks and
        swings,
An eagle alit one moment may sit
    In the light of its golden wings.
And when Sunset may breathe, from
    the lit sea beneath,
    Its ardors of rest and of love,
And the crimson pall of eve may fall
    From the depth of Heaven above,
With wings folded I rest, on mine airy
    nest,
    As still as a brooding dove.

That orbèd maiden with white fire lad-
    en,
    Whom mortals call the Moon,
Glides glimmering o'er my fleecelike
    floor,
    By the midnight breezes strewn;

And wherever the beat of her unseen
    feet,
    Which only the angels hear,
May have broken the woof of my tent's
    thin roof,
    The stars peep behind her and peer;
And I laugh to see them whirl and flee,
    Like a swarm of golden bees,
When I widen the rent in my wind-built
    tent,
    Till the calm rivers, lakes, and seas,
Like strips of the sky fallen through me
    on high,
    Are each paved with the moon and
    these.

I bind the Sun's throne with a burning
    zone,
    And the Moon's with a girdle of pearl;
The volcanoes are dim, and the stars
    reel and swim
    When the whirlwinds my banner un-
    furl.
From cape to cape, with a bridgelike
    shape,
    Over a torrent sea,
Sunbeam-proof, I hang like a roof —
    The mountains its columns be.
The triumphal arch through which I
    march
    With hurricane, fire, and snow,
When the Powers of the air are chained
    to my chair,
    Is the million-colored bow;
The sphere fire above its soft colors
    wove,
    While the moist Earth was laughing
    below.

I am the daughter of Earth and Water,
    And the nursling of the Sky;
I pass through the pores of the ocean
    and shores,
    I change, but I cannot die.
For after the rain when with never a
    stain
The pavilion of Heaven is bare,
And the winds and sunbeams with their
    convex gleams
    Build up the blue dome of air,

I silently laugh at my own cenotaph,
    And out of the caverns of rain,
Like a child from the womb, like a
    ghost from the tomb,
    I arise and unbuild it again.

Focus on Meaning

1. Roberts describes the heron and its surroundings with words. Try to imagine the poem as a painting or a photograph. What do you see first? How has the artist used colours? After studying the painting for a while, what will you remember the most?

2. What mood does Lampman create in his sonnet? How does he do this?

3. Wordsworth's poem "I Wandered Lonely as a Cloud" conveys a very vivid experience. What is his experience? Have you ever had a similar one?

4. The last line of the poem "Snow" is an intriguing statement. It pertains to the poem, obviously, but it is also a statement to consider, beyond the poem. Think about the statement. Then write a creative composition, which begins, "There is more than glass between the snow and the huge roses."

5. What do you find particularly descriptive about Emily Dickinson's poem? What is your overall impression of this poem?

6. Arrange a presentation in which you accompany a reading of the poem "The Cloud" with appropriate background music and slides. You may want to have the reading in more than one voice, or vary from solo to choral work. You could enhance the many beautiful images in the poem with slides and artistic movement from one slide to the next. Put on your interpretive reading for your classmates, or invite another class to your reading/showing.

7. Nature poetry is rich in seasonal imagery. What seasons are explored by the poems in this chapter? What various moods are created? What poems do you find most effective? Why?

21 Reflection

A good poem may be written about anything. In this chapter, the range of topics includes a flight of wild swans, a plowman, a quiet room, a frightened mouse, a collection of holy books, and a pile of rocks. Elsewhere, we can read of everything from kisses to coffins to clouds.

A good poet doesn't ignore the ordinary. In poems we are often encouraged to see things we have seen before but through new eyes, in new ways. We are encouraged to reflect upon the ordinary but also to go beyond it.

Thus, a poem may move us with imagery, may inspire us with noble themes, but also challenge us to go deeper than its surface. Something ordinary becomes something new. Through the poem, we experience a moment of insight. This is reflection.

The Rock Pile
Fred Cogswell

Right in the middle of a field there stands
A huge rockpile, but most of it is one
Big stone, a lump of rock that weighs a ton
Or more, too much for horses or for hands
To budge, and there the man who cleared these lands,
Jim Armstrong, in the days of brawn and grit
Wrestled for weeks in vain to lever it;
It broke his harness, traces, grappling bands.

And so Jim covered up with little stones
The only thing in life he could not beat;
But when new settlers came after a while
To look and praise in awed, admiring tones
The mighty rockpile in his field, he'd smile
A twisted smile and find the credit sweet.

In the Street
Dorothy Livesay

In rainy weather
Who can tell
Whether we weep
Or not?

I dread the sun
For his fierce honesty.

The Plowman
Raymond Knister

All day I follow
Watching the swift dark furrow
That curls away before me,
And care not for skies or upturned flowers,
And at the end of the field
Look backward
Ever with discontent.
A stone, a root, a strayed thought
Has warped the line of that furrow —
And urge my horses 'round again.

Sometimes even before the row is finished
I must look backward;
To find, when I come to the end
That there I swerved.

Unappeased I leave the field,
Expectant, return.

The horses are very patient.
When I tell myself
This time
The ultimate unflawed turning
Is before my share,
They must give up their rest.

Someday, someday, be sure,
I shall turn the furrow of all my hopes
But I shall not, doing it, look backward.

Modern Ode to the Modern School
John Erskine

Just after the Board had brought the schools up to date
To prepare you for your Life Work
Without teaching you one superfluous thing,
Jim Reilly presented himself to be educated.
He wanted to be a bricklayer.
They taught him to be a perfect bricklayer.
And nothing more.

He knew so much about bricklaying
That the contractor made him a foreman
But he knew nothing about being a foreman.
He spoke to the School Board about it,
And they put in a night course
On how to be a foreman
And nothing more.

He became so excellent a foreman
That the contractor made him a partner.
But he knew nothing about figuring costs
Nor about bookkeeping
Nor about real estate,
And he was too proud to go back to night school.
So he hired a tutor
Who taught him these things
And nothing more.

Prospering at last
And meeting other men as prosperous,
Whenever the conversation started, he'd say to himself
"Just wait till it comes my way —
Then I'll show them!"
But they never mentioned bricklaying
Nor the art of being a foreman
Nor the whole duty of contractors,
Nor even real estate.
So Jim never said anything.

New Year's Poem
Margaret Avison

The Christmas twigs crispen and needles rattle
Along the windowledge.
          A solitary pearl
Shed from the necklace spilled at last week's party
Lies in the suety, snow-luminous plainness
Of morning, on the windowledge beside them.
And all the furniture that circled stately
And hospitable when these rooms were brimmed
With perfumes, furs, and black-and-silver
Crisscross of seasonal conversation, lapses
Into its previous largeness.
          I remember
Anne's rose-sweet gravity, and the stiff grave
Where cold so little can contain;
I mark the queer delightful skull and crossbones
Starlings and sparrows left, taking the crust,
And the long loop of winter wind
Smoothing its arc from dark Arcturus down
To the bricked corner of the drifted courtyard,
And the still windowledge.
          Gentle and just pleasure
It is, being human, to have won from space
This unchill, habitable interior
Which mirrors quietly the light
Of the snow, and the new year.

Wild Swans
Edna St. Vincent Millay

I looked in my heart while the wild swans went
     over.
And what did I see I had not seen before?
Only a question less or a question more;
Nothing to match the flight of wild birds flying.
Tiresome heart, forever living and dying,
House without air, I leave you and lock your door.
Wild swans, come over the town, come over
The town again, trailing your legs and crying!

To a Mouse
Robert Burns

Wee, sleekit, cowrin', tim'rous beastie,
O, what a panic's in thy breastie!
Thou need na start awa sae hasty
   Wi' bickering brattle!
I wad be laith to rin an' chase thee
   Wi' murd'rin' pattle!

I'm truly sorry man's dominion
Has broken nature's social union,
An' justifies that ill opinion
   Which makes thee startle
At me, thy poor, earthborn companion,
   An' fellow mortal!

I doubt na, whyles, but thou may thieve;
What then? poor beastie, thou maun
     live!
A daimen icker in a thrave
   'S a sma' request;
I'll get a blessin' wi' the lave,
   An' never miss 't!

Thy wee bit housie, too, in ruin!
It's silly wa's the win's are strewin'!
An' naething, now, to big a new ane,
   O' foggage green!
An' bleak December's winds ensuin',
   Baith snell an' keen!

Thou saw the fields laid bare and waste,
An' weary winter comin' fast,
An' cozie here, beneath the blast,
   Thou thought to dwell,
Till crash! the cruel coulter passed
   Out through thy cell.

That wee bit heap o' leaves an' stibble
Has cost thee mony a weary nibble!
Now thou's turn'd out, for a' thy trouble,
   But house or hald,
To thole the winter's sleety dribble
   An' cranreuch cauld!

But, Mousie, thou art no thy lane
In proving foresight may be vain;
The best laid schemes o' mice an' men
   Gang aft agley,
An' lea'e us nought but grief an' pain,
   For promis'd joy.

Still thou art blest, compared wi' me,
The present only toucheth thee;
But och! I backward cast my e'e
   On prospects drear!
An' forward, though I canna see,
   I guess an' fear!

Heirloom
A. M. Klein

My father bequeathed me no wide estates;
No keys and ledgers were my heritage;
Only some holy books with *yahrzeit* dates
Writ mournfully upon a blank front page —

Books of the Baal Shem Tov, and of his wonders;
Pamphlets upon the devil and his crew;
Prayers against road demons, witches, thunders;
And sundry other tomes for a good Jew.

Beautiful: though no pictures on them, save
The scorpion crawling on a printed track;
The Virgin floating on a scriptural wave,
Square letters twinkling in the Zodiac.

The snuff left on this page, now brown and old,
The tallow stains of midnight liturgy —
These are my coat of arms, and these unfold
My noble lineage, my proud ancestry!

And my tears, too, have stained this heirloomed ground,
When reading in these treatises some weird
Miracle, I turned a leaf and found
A white hair fallen from my father's beard.

Ode On Solitude

Alexander Pope

Happy the man whose wish and care
    A few paternal acres bound,
Content to breathe his native air
    In his own ground.

Whose herds with milk, whose fields with bread,
    Whose flocks supply him with attire,
Whose trees in summer yield him shade,
    In winter fire.

Bless'd who can unconcern'dly find
    Hours, days, and years slide soft away,
In health of body, peace of mind,
    Quiet by day;

Sound sleep by night: study and ease
    Together mix'd; sweet recreation;
And innocence, which most does please,
    With Meditation.

Thus let me live, unseen, unknown,
    Thus unlamented let me die;
Steal from the world, and not a stone
    Tell where I lie.

Focus on Meaning

1. What details does Fred Cogswell supply about Jim Armstrong in "The Rock Pile"? What else can you learn about him from reading between the lines of the poem? Have you met anyone like Jim in your own life? from reading other literature? Write a short character sketch about him or her.

2. It seems that Knister is using the experience of plowing in "The Plowman" to reflect on something deeper. What is Knister saying?

3. a) Explain the poet's purpose in "Modern Ode to the Modern School."
   b) Write a paragraph in which you compare your education with that of Jim Reilly. Do you think your present education will leave gaps in your knowledge? If so, what gaps? What can you do about it?

4. In "New Year's Poem," what tangible things spark the poet's remembrances? What does she remember? These lead her to a reflection. What is that reflection? Have you ever felt the way the poet feels?

5. In "Wild Swans," what do the wild swans cause the poet to question in herself? What do the wild swans represent? Can you think of other images or symbols the poet might have used for the same effect?

6. Practise reading "To a Mouse" out loud, using your best Scottish accent. What other examples of literature written in dialect can you find? Bring these to class and experiment reading these out loud as well.

7. How do the books in "Heirloom" represent a heritage for the poet? Why? In your own life, what is your heritage? Is there an article or a possession which for you represents this heritage? Explain.

8. According to Pope's "Ode on Solitude," what makes him happy? What does he want out of life? Do you agree or disagree with him? Write a paragraph in which you express what you want out of your life.

In 1818, Keats nursed his brother Tom who was dying of tuberculosis. During this time, he also fell in love with the beautiful actress Fanny Brawne. They became engaged, but it was a desperate relationship, for Keats was dedicated to his poetry, was too poor to marry, and, worst of all, was also suffering from tuberculosis and therefore dying. In the autumn of 1820, he went to Italy in hopes that the warmer climate would cure him, but on February 23, 1821, he died in Rome.

At Keats' request, his grave is marked with the words: "Here lies one whose name was writ in water." It seems that he thought he had failed in his poetry and in his life. History has proved him wrong, for, in spite of the fact that his genius was ended by his early death, his work today holds a high place in English poetry.

Junkets

Alden Nowlan

You magnificent
redhaired runt!

I wish I could
telephone you
right now
and ask you over.

I've got a new
second-hand pinball
machine.

There's gin.

And we could
send out for
Chinese food,
if you liked.

I don't suppose
you've ever tasted it.

But you're so
far away.
I could never
reach you.

And even if
you were here
in town
I'd be afraid
of intruding:
I'm like that.

Worst of all,
it would never
work,
Junkets:

I'd keep thinking,
dear God,

I'm talking
with John Keats.

John Keats was a Londoner. Born over a London stable, the son of a stable-keeper, his beginnings were much humbler than those of his contemporaries, Byron and Shelley, who were both aristocrats. Nor was Keats sent to the best schools, although he received an education in a small private school at Enfield.

At fifteen Keats was apprenticed to a surgeon and apothecary. Five years later he continued his studies at Guy's Hospital, London, but then chose to abandon a career in medicine for poetry. Between the ages of twenty-two and twenty-five, Keats published three books of poetry. These poems show his love for nature, his integrity, his common sense. They reveal a poet who is deeply thoughtful, and, especially in the earlier poems, a poet with a deep sense of joy.

*Junkets was a nickname of John Keats, given him by Leigh Hunt, an incorrigible maker of puns.

This Living Hand

This living hand, now warm and capable
Of earnest grasping, would, if it were cold
And in the icy silence of the tomb,
So haunt thy days and chill thy dreaming nights
That thou wouldst wish thine own heart dry of blood
So in my veins red life might stream again,
And thou be conscience-calmed — see here it is —
I hold it towards you.

To One Who Has Been Long in City Pent

To one who has been long in city pent,
  'Tis very sweet to look into the fair
  And open face of heaven, — to breathe a prayer
Full in the smile of the blue firmament.
Who is more happy, when, with heart's content,
  Fatigued he sinks into some pleasant lair
  Of wavy grass, and reads a debonair
And gentle tale of love and languishment?
Returning home at evening, with an ear
  Catching the notes of Philomel, — an eye
Watching the sailing cloudlet's bright career,
  He mourns that day so soon has glided by:
E'en like the passage of an angel's tear
  That falls through the clear ether silently.

Ode to Autumn

Season of mists and mellow fruitfulness,
  Close bosom-friend of the maturing sun;
Conspiring with him how to load and bless
  With fruit the vines that round the thatch-eves run;
To bend with apples the mossed cottage-trees,
  And fill all fruit with ripeness to the core;
    To swell the gourd, and plump the hazel shells
  With a sweet kernel; to set budding more,
And still more, later flowers for the bees,
Until they think warm days will never cease,
    For Summer has o'er-brimmed their clammy cells.

Who hath not seen thee oft amid thy store?
  Sometimes whoever seeks abroad may find
Thee sitting careless on a granary floor,
  Thy hair soft-lifted by the winnowing wind;
Or on a half-reaped furrow sound asleep,
  Drowsed with the fume of poppies, while thy hook
    Spares the next swath and all its twinéd flowers:
And sometimes like a gleaner thou dost keep
  Steady thy laden head across a brook;
  Or by a cider-press, with patient look,
    Thou watchest the last oozings hours by hours.

Where are the songs of Spring? Ay, where are they?
  Think not of them, thou hast thy music too, —
While barred clouds bloom the soft-dying day,
  And touch the stubble-plains with rosy hue;
Then in a wailful choir the small gnats mourn
  Among the river sallows borne aloft
  Or sinking as the light wind lives or dies;
And full-grown lambs loud bleat from hilly bourn;
  Hedge-crickets sing; and now with treble soft
  The red-breast whistles from a garden-croft;
    And gathering swallows twitter in the skies.

La Belle Dame Sans Merci

O what can ail thee, knight-at-arms,
    Alone and palely loitering?
The sedge has withered from the lake,
    And no birds sing.

O what can ail thee, knight-at-arms!
    So haggard and so woe-begone?
The squirrel's granary is full,
    And the harvest's done.

I see a lily on thy brow,
    With anguish moist and fever dew,
And on thy cheeks a fading rose
    Fast withereth too.

I met a lady in the meads,
    Full beautiful — a faery's child,
Her hair was long, her foot was light,
    And her eyes were wild.

I made a garland for her head,
    And bracelets too, and fragrant zone;
She looked at me as she did love,
    And made sweet moan.

I set her on my pacing steed,
    And nothing else saw all day long,
For sidelong would she bend, and sing
    A faery's song.

She found me roots of relish sweet,
    And honey wild, and manna dew,
And sure in language strange she said —
    "I love thee true."

She took me to her elfin grot,
    And there she wept, and sighed full sore,
And there I shut her wild wild eyes
    With kisses four.

And there she lullèd me asleep,
    And there I dreamed — Ah! woe betide!
The latest dream I ever dreamed
    On the cold hill side.

I saw pale kings and princes too,
    Pale warriors, death-pale were they all;
They cried — "La Belle Dame sans Merci
    Hath thee in thrall!"

I saw their starved lips in the gloam,
    With horrid warning gapèd wide,
And I awoke and found me here,
    On the cold hill's side.

And this is why I sojourn here,
    Alone and palely loitering,
Though the sedge has withered from the lake,
    And no birds sing.

Focus on John Keats

1. "This Living Hand" is a brief fragment of poetry written for Fanny Brawne. What feelings does it stir in you? How do you think Fanny Brawne might have reacted to it?

2. What conventional ideas and images are often associated with autumn? How do you think Keats has gone beyond these in his "Ode to Autumn"?

3. "La Belle Dame Sans Merci" is Keats' version of the traditional ballad, "Thomas the Rhymer." How has Keats changed that story?

4. Write a short skit in which you dramatize an event, real or imaginary, in the life of John Keats. For example, you could dramatize a moment from his childhood, or his farewell to Fanny as he leaves for Italy, or a moment during the writing of one of his poems. Perhaps you could artistically incorporate some lines from Keats' poetry into your skit.

Earle Birney was born in Calgary, Alberta, and educated at the Universities of British Columbia, Toronto, and London. His career as a university professor has taken him throughout Canada and the world. Similarly, his poems take the reader from the Canadian countryside Birney knows so well, all the way around the globe. His poems are universal — it seems as though they could happen anywhere, anytime. For the past few years Birney has been Professor of English at the University of British Columbia, where he has instituted the Department of Creative Writing.

The major themes of Birney's work often deal with a criticism of contemporary society and the contrast of people's aims and their achievements. These themes appear in both traditional and experimental forms. He handles traditional forms like lyrics and narratives with great skill — witness the verbal magic of such beloved classics as "Bear on the Delhi Road" and "David." Lately, however, it appears that Birney's creative emphasis has been on a more experimental form of verse. Perhaps he feels that for the purpose of expressing certain emotions, sensations, or creative instincts, the traditional poetry maintains a spirit of perpetual youth in his verse. Nevertheless, whether his poems are traditional or experimental in form, they achieve superlative moods of serenity, humour, irony, tenderness, and hope.

Twice a winner of the Governor General's Award and the author of twenty-three volumes of poetry, fiction, criticism, anthologies, and editions, as well as nearly one hundred short stories, pamphlets, essays, reviews, and articles, Birney has contributed immeasurably to Canadian poetry.

The Bear on the Delhi Road

Unreal, tall as a myth
by the road the Himalayan bear
is beating the brilliant air
with his crooked arms.
About him two men, bare,
spindly as locusts, leap.
One pulls on a ring
in the great soft nose; his mate
flicks, flicks with a stick
up at the rolling eyes.

They have not led him here,
down from the fabulous hills
to this bald, alien plain
and the clamorous world, to kill
but simply to teach him to dance.

They are peaceful both, these spare
men of Kashmir, and the bear
alive is their living too.
If far on the Delhi way
around him galvanic they dance
it is merely to wear, wear
from his shaggy body the tranced
wish forever to stay
only an ambling bear
four-footed in berries.

It is no more joyous for them
in this hot dust to prance
out of reach of the praying claws
sharpened to paw for ants
in the shadows of deodars.
It is not easy to free
myth from reality
or rear this fellow up
to lurch, lurch with them
in the tranced dancing of men.

Daybreak on Lake Opal: High Rockies

as
the
fire
from
opals
a trem
-ulous
dawn be-
gins its
ceremony of
s l o w touch
without palms
its breath with-
out breathing along
the whorled turrets
moving shimmering fall
-ing over the scarred for
-ever-by-the-wind-besieged
ramparts the icecracked tree-
breached walls   the light of
the untouchable Sun sliding from
skyblue into the chill broken flesh
of our lifedrop   warming freeing the
silence of jays and firtops   sending a
heather of wind over unfolding asters and
eaglets   ruffling the moated lake to a green
soul and rolling once more the upraised sacrifice
of our world into the sword of Its   P R E S E N C E

Winter Saturday

Furred from the farmhouse
like the caterpillars from wood
they emerge, the storm blown out,
and find in the Ford their cocoon.
Through hardening dusk and over
the cold void impelled, they move
to dreams of light and sound.
Over drifts like headlands they go,
drawn to the town's pink cloud,
gliding unamazed through snow
by the wind marbled and fluted.

With tentacle headlights now
they feel the watertank, grope
with Main Street, are blissfully caught.
Hatch from the car like trembling moths,
circle to faces, flutter to movie,
throb through the dance in a sultry swoon.
But lights fail, time is false,
the town was less than its glow.
Again in chrysalis folded
they must go lonely
drowsy back through ghosts
the wind starts from the waiting snow.

Focus on Earle Birney

1. Of the writing of "The Bear on the Delhi Road," Earle Birney once said:

   "In the summer of 1958 I had a glimpse of a bear and two Kashmiri men on a roadside in northern India — seen from my passing car. It was a strange sight, of course, but it haunted me for reasons far beyond oddness . . . . Bear and men pursued me for fourteen months till I could find the leisure on a Mediterranean island, and the mood, — and then in two hours the words came and the bearish rhythm and the images to lay those three ghosts, which were I think also the ghosts of my multitudinous guilt feelings, as a well-fed western tourist in a world of unimaginable poverty and heat and dusty slaving."

   After you've read Birney's comments on this poem, could you put in your own words what you think the poet is trying to say? In your answer you might consider the following questions.

   - What is the human/animal relationship described?
   - What haunted the poet most — the wretchedness of the bear or the wretchedness of the men?
   - Why do the two men and the bear remain in Birney's mind (as "ghosts") long after he has seen them?
   - Why does the poet have "guilt feelings"?
   - How does the predicament of the men and the bear arouse various feelings — compassion, fear, love, despair — in the poet?

2. What do you think of "shape poetry" like "Daybreak on Lake Opal: High Rockies"? Why do you think this type of poetry is effective or ineffective?

Index of First Lines

Index of Titles

U

V

W

Page 95 — *nobody loses all the time* reprinted from IS 5 POEMS by e.e. cummings by permission of Liveright Publishing Corporation. Copyright 1926 by Horace Liveright. Copyright renewed 1953 by e.e. cummings. *Page 96* — *Waiter! . . . There's an Alligator in My Coffee* from TOP SOIL, Reprinted by permission of the author. *Page 98* — *Flight of the Roller Coaster, The Top Hat* by Raymond Souster from THE COLOUR OF THE TIMES by permission of Oberon Press; *Orange Butterfly Lighting* by Raymond Souster from HANGING IN by permission of Oberon Press. *Page 99* — *Our Weeping-Willow* by Raymond Souster from HANGING IN by permission of Oberon Press. *Page 102* — *The Taxi* from THE COMPLETE POETICAL WORKS OF AMY LOWELL. Copyright © 1955 by Houghton Mifflin Company. Reprinted by permission of the publisher. *Page 103* — *For Anne* from THE SPICE BOX OF EARTH reprinted by permission of The Canadian Publishers, McClelland and Stewart, Limited, Toronto; *Psyche with the Candle* from NEW AND COLLECTED POEMS 1917-1976 by Archibald MacLeish, Copyright © 1976 by Archibald MacLeish. Reprinted by permission of Houghton Mifflin Company. *Page 104* — *Love Is Not All* from COLLECTED POEMS, Harper & Row. Copyright 1921, 1931, 1948, 1958 by Edna St. Vincent Millay and Norma Millay Ellis. *Page 105* — *Memory* from FIGURES IN A LANDSCAPE. By permission of Oberon Press; *Song for Naomi* from THE COLLECTED POEMS OF IRVING LAYTON reprinted by permission of The Canadian Publishers, McClelland and Stewart Limited, Toronto. *Page 106* — *Journey of the Magi* from COLLECTED POEMS 1909-1962, by T.S. Eliot. Reprinted by permission of Faber and Faber, Ltd. *Page 107* — *When You Are Old* from COLLECTED POEMS by W.B. Yeats Reprinted by permission of M.B. Yeats, Anne Yeats and MacMillan London Limited, Reprinted with permission of MacMillan Publishing Co., Inc. from COLLECTED POEMS of William Butler Yeats (New York: Macmillan, 1956); *Remember* from POETICAL WORKS OF CHRISTINA G. ROSSETTI (New York: MacMillan, 1924); *The Circle Game* © 1966 Siquomb Publishing Corporation Used by permission. All rights reserved. *Page 108* — *Elegy: The Wood Is Bare* from A GATHERING OF POEMS. Reprinted by permission of Pocket Books Inc. *Page 110* — *The Coffins* For permission to include "The Coffins" from POEMS, by James Reaney, New Press, Toronto, copyright Canada 1972, thanks are due to the author, New Press, Publisher, and Sybil Hutchinson, Literary Agent; *Do Not Go Gentle into That Good Night* from THE COLLECTED POEMS OF DYLAN THOMAS. Reprinted by permission of J.M. Dent Limited. Dylan Thomas, THE POEMS OF DYLAN THOMAS. Copyright 1952 by Dylan Thomas; *Erosion* Reprinted by permission of Viola and Claire Pratt and the Pratt Estate. *Page 111* — *The Soldier* Reprinted by permission of Dodd, Mead & Company, Inc. from THE COLLECTED POEMS OF RUPERT BROOKE. Copyright 1915 by Dodd, Mead & Company, Inc. Copyright renewed 1943 by Edward Marsh. From COLLECTED POEMS by Rupert Brooke reprinted by permission of The Canadian Publishers, McClelland and Stewart Limited, Toronto; *In Flanders Fields* Reproduced by permission of Punch. *Page 112* — *The Fox* from Collected Poems. Copyright 1939 by New Directions Publishing Corporation. Reprinted by permission of New Directions Publishing Corporation. *Page 113* — *The Blue Heron* from THE LEATHER BOTTLE by Theodore G. Roberts. Reprinted by permission of McGraw-Hill Ryerson Limited. *Page 114* — *A November Landscape* Reprinted by permission of Viola and Claire Pratt and the Pratt Estate; *Velvet Shoes* Copyright 1921 by Alfred A. Knopf, Inc. and renewed 1949 by William Rose Benet. Reprinted from COLLECTED POEMS OF ELINOR WYLIE, by Elinor Wylie, by permission of Alfred A. Knopf, Inc.; *Snow* Reprinted by permission of Faber and Faber Ltd. from THE COLLECTED POEMS OF LOUIS MACNEICE. *Page 115* — *A Bird Came Down the Walk* Reprinted by permission of the publishers and the trustees of Amherst College from *The Poems of Emily Dickinson*, edited by Thomas H. Johnson, Cambridge, Mass: The Belknap Press of Harvard University Press, Copyright 1951, © 1955, 1979 by the President and Fellows of Harvard College; *The Cloud* from THE COMPLETE WORKS OF PERCY BYSSHE SHELLEY. Reprinted by permission of Ernest Benn Limited. *Page 117* — *The Rock Pile* by permission of the author; *In the Street* from POETS BETWEEN THE WARS Milton Wilson ed. McClelland and Stewart Copyright Dorothy Livesay; *The Plowman* from THE COLLECTED POEMS OF RAYMOND KNISTER. Reprinted by permission of McGraw-Hill Ryerson Limited. *Page 118* — *New Year's Poem* from POETRY OF MID-CENTURY 1940-1960 by Margaret Avison. Reprinted by permission of The Canadian Publishers McClelland and Stewart Limited, Toronto; *Wild Swans* from Collected Poems, Harper and Row, Copyright 1921, 1931, 1948, 1958 by Edna St. Vincent Millay and Norma Millay Ellis. *Page 119* — *Heirloom* from THE COLLECTED POEMS OF A.M. KLEIN. Reprinted by permission of McGraw-Hill Ryerson Limited. *Page 126* — *the witch* House of Anansi Press for "the witch" by Terrence Heath, *the truth and other stories* (1972). *Page 127* — *anyone lived in a pretty how town* from COMPLETE POEMS: 1913-1962 by e.e. cummings. *Page 128* — *Billy the Kid* by permission of the author. *Page 129* — *Ukrainian Church* from Driving Home by Miriam Waddington © Oxford University Press, Canada. *Page 130* — *Mountain Lion* Copyright © 1964 The Estate of Frieda Lawrence Ravagli from THE COMPLETE POEMS OF D.H. LAWRENCE. Acknowledgement is also given to Laurence Pollinger Ltd., and the estate of Frieda Lawrence Ravagli; by D.H. Lawrence, from THE COMPLETE POEMS OF D.H. LAWRENCE, Collected and edited with an Introduction and Notes by Vivian de Sola Pinto and F. Warren Roberts. Copyright 1967, 1971 by Angelo Ravagli and C.M. Weekley, as executors of the estate of Frieda Lawrence Ravagli. Reprinted by permission of Viking Penguin, Inc. *Page 131* — *The Diver* from SHAPES AND SOUNDS: POEMS OF W.W.E. ROSS by W.W.E. Ross, Academic Press Canada. *Page 132* — *The Future of Poetry in Canada* from SUNRISE NORTH By Elizabeth Brewster © 1972 by Clarke, Irwin & Company Limited Used by permission. *Page 133* — *constantly risking absurdity* Lawrence Ferlinghetti, A CONEY ISLAND OF THE MIND. Copyright © 1958 by Lawrence Ferlinghetti Reprinted by permission of New Directions Publishing Corporation. *Page 134* — *Portrait of Marina* reprinted by permission of the author; *Wild Horses* from POEMS, NEW AND SELECTED, Oxford University Press. Reprinted by permission of the author. *Page 135* — *The Sculptors* from North of Summer by Al Purdy reprinted by permission of The Canadian Publishers, McClelland and Stewart Limited, Toronto. *Page 136* — *th tomato conspiracy aint worth a whol pome* reprinted from BEYOND EVEN FAITHFUL LEGENDS Talonbooks 1980 by permission of the author. *Page 137* — *This Is Just to Say* William Carlos Williams, COLLECTED EARLIER POEMS OF WILLIAM CARLOS WILLIAMS. Copyright 1938 by New Directions Publishing Corporation; *Pear Tree* H.D., SELECTED POEMS OF H.D. Copyright 1925, 1953, 1957 by Norman Holmes Pearson Reprinted by permission of New Directions Publishing Corporation. *Page 138* — *The Fish* reprinted by permission of Farrar, Straus and Giroux, Inc. "The Fish" from ELIZABETH BISHOP: THE COMPLETE POEMS. Copyright © 1940, 1969 by Elizabeth Bishop. *Page 139* — *A London Thoroughfare, Two A.M.* from THE COMPLETE POETICAL WORKS OF AMY LOWELL. Copyright © 1955 by Houghton Mifflin Company. Reprinted by permission of the publisher. *Page 142* — *Mirror* Copyright © 1957 by John Updike. Reprinted from THE CARPENTERED HEN AND OTHER TAME CREATURES, by John Updike, by permission of Alfred A. Knopf, Inc. *Page 144* — *This Is a Poem* by permission of the author © Paul Dutton, 1975. *Page 145* — *The Bear on the Delhi Road* from The Collected Poems of Earle Birney reprinted by permission of The Canadian Publishers, McClelland and Stewart Limited, Toronto. *Page 146* — *Daybreak on Lake Opal: High Rockies, Winter Saturday* from GHOST IN THE WHEELS reprinted by permission of The Canadian Publishers, McClelland and Stewart Limited, Toronto.

Every effort has been made to trace and acknowledge the holders of copyright material used in this book. The authors and publisher apologize for any errors or omissions in acknowledgements. Any such errors brought to our attention will be noted and corrected in future editions.